The Extreme Center

The Extreme Center

NELS F.S. FERRÉ

WORD BOOKS, Publishers
Waco, Texas

Library of Congress catalog card number: 73–84581
Printed in the United States of America

Contents

5

Preface

PREACHING IS A PRIVILEGE and an art. I have enjoyed the privilege although I am far from mastering the art. History shows, however, that some theologians have put their best thought into sermons where it is more generally available. Thus a book of sermons or sermon-essays is not only for ministers, who share the craft and the message, but also for laymen for their devotional reading and even for students of theology who may be interested in particular aspects of a theologian's thought.

This collection of sermons exemplifies varied kinds of preaching. One approach uses a complete manuscript ready for publication. Another makes use of full notes with an informal delivery. Both are needed for their purposes, the former, as for instance "The Age of Unimunity," given at Princeton University Chapel. The latter ministers to a more varied congregation, as one might find at Chautauqua, where the majority of these sermons were preached. Informal sermons, to be sure, are humbling for a writer to see in print, but experience shows that they often help the most. One sermon, frankly, was an experiment. An invitation from the chapel committee of Harvard Divinity School to preach on the entire Sermon on the Mount baffled me at first as an impossible assignment; the result of much prayer and study shows one way of preaching on a large block of Scripture.

With regard to preaching from the Bible, the book aims at being biblical while avoiding as the plague all biblicism. Biblicism is the exegesis of separate texts of the Bible apart from their meaning in the light of the total context of the Bible's highest and fullest message. The relation between biblical interpretation

7

and biblicism which I employ (depending technically upon the right relationship between hermeneutics and exegesis) is carefully developed in Chapter III of *The Living God of Nowhere and Nothing*, "The Bible and the Book of God." We must have freedom not only to find the truth in the Bible but also to use the Bible in behalf of all needed and relevant truth. The nature of the "larger logic of the Bible" entails such an approach.

The sermon on "unimunity" is set apart from the rest because it is the first sermonic expression of my life task, set forth in *The Universal Word*, to change our very framework of thought in line with the biblical categories at their deepest. My aim is to release the fullness of the biblical base of truth as such. I am convinced that a new day of biblical light and living, beyond our past cramped biblicisms, is ready to break.

The message and the response are universal. Tokyo Union and a rural church in Japan, a Chinese church in Hong Kong, a community church and a university church in India, an Arab Christian church and the American University of Beirut Chapel, City Temple in London, College chapels of the University of London or Cambridge University, St. Cuthbert's or Wellington or a "scientific" congregation in a small experimental city in Scotland, Harvard University's Memorial Church or a rural congregation in Iowa—all human beings are *most deeply the same* and respond alike to the eternal riches and reality of the gospel.

Four of these sermons, "Heritage and History," "A Future and a Hope," "The Age of Unimunity," and "Living Truth" appeared in *The Pulpit;* "Extremism Without Extremity" in Britain in *The Expository Times*. Many of my most treasured letters in response to published sermons surprise me by the varied backgrounds of the readers. The world seems hungry for the message. If only we could better master and manage the medium.

I send out *The Extreme Center* with a believing prayer and hope that through these sermons many will find a new depth of personal living and a fuller vision, urgency and expectation of the new age of the Spirit which can be nothing less than the age of universal man.

NELS F. S. FERRÉ

PART I
Old Testament

1.
Heritage and History

> *I did not send the prophets, yet they ran; I did
> not speak to them, yet they prophesied. But if they
> had stood in my council, then they would have
> proclaimed my words to my people, and they would
> have turned them from their evil way, and from the
> evil of their doings.* Jeremiah 23:21–22.

JEREMIAH WAS heartbroken because of the prophets. They ran, but
they were not sent; they prophesied, but gave only their own
opinion. They never stood in God's council but learned mostly
from each other and from dreams. Therefore the false prophets
were God's real burden.

The prophets, too, kept pointing back to God's original deliverance of the people from the land of Egypt, but they did not trust
him to deliver his people from their present exile in the north
country. Today the false prophet extols first-century Christianity
and God's mighty deeds in the Reformation; the true prophet ex-
pects God to deliver us, as we repent and reform, from our present national corruption and from atomic catastrophe. The false
prophet glories in past ages; the true, in God's new age.

I

Even though the false prophet centers his message in the past,
no true prophet can forget the heritage of the people. He, too,
must be thankful for the past and remind his people of God's
mighty deeds in the long ago. No true prophet, even in confront-

11

ing the present, neglects the past. History must be rooted in
heritage.

One of our problems today is rootlessness, first of all in the
case of the Christian faith. Modern educated man no longer swallows Christian ideology. For him it has become a strange tale.
Some suffer from the loss; others feel freed by it. But deep down
they all experience rootlessness.

I heard a New England college professor of physics tell how
life shaking it had been for him to give up his native Kentucky
fundamentalism for modern scientism. Now he would like to end
each academic year by telling his classes to forget all about the
Christian faith. "But," said he, "I don't feel religiously at home
anywhere. The liberal churches sicken me. They have no
'oomph.'" He felt rootless.

In Japan I saw Christians who were rootless because they had
left the Buddhist faith, but one church adapted to its use the
Buddhist festival that celebrates ancestors' day. At the front of the
sanctuary there were displayed rows of photographs of church
members who had died, some recently, some in years past. As the
name of the deceased was called, the family or a representative
would go forward, bow deeply toward the picture in dignified
Japanese style, stand reverently for a few moments in honoring
meditation, and bow again as in leave-taking before returning
to the seat. Somehow this simple act went back to the people's
religious roots and filled a deep need in their lives.

But the Christian heritage does not stand alone. Especially for
those of us who belong to the academic community there is the
heritage of scientism. Notice I did not say "science." Legitimate
science deals with facts, with differing methods according to vary-
ing fields of inquiry. Science never constructs world views. When
world views are made in the name of science they lack both the
sanction and the spirit of science. Such world views scientism as
a faith creates.

Man cannot live without interpreting the whole of his experience. Such an interpretation can never be checked or proved entirely. Whatever view we have to make then should contain as
much fact as possible and be built with all possible critical care of
thought and imagination. But scientism was the reductionistic

faith of a naturalistic philosophy which in general accepted evolution, not only as a description of creation but as a total explanation of how the world and history have come to be. Such a world view is far more fantastic in its assumptions than any Christian fundamentalism with a once-for-all creation and axheads floating in rivers.

At least the traditional Christian faith posited creative Being as the ground and goal of nature and history. Thus it satisfied the requirements of reason to the extent that the history of the natural and the human world had adequate cause and purpose. Such theology contained much unfactual data and gross immoral elements, but as a whole it hung together and gave unity and drive to man's life.

Scientism, however, begged the whole question of both cause and purpose. Reductionistic naturalism, disclaiming all reality and direction beyond the natural processes, was a mystique so fantastic that it is hard to believe any hard-headed thinker could have fallen prey to it. Yet such fundamentalistic scientism reigned supreme throughout most academic life over many generations, coming to a climax early in our century.

Today scientism is dead or dying. The optimistic faith in progress as inherent in process has been put already in the museum of religious relics. Darwinian evolutionism, one of its examples, is now held only by reactionary fanatics unwilling to face the fact that science is positivistic—that is, science deals with fact only on the level of fact and not on the level of faith. Even mechanistic determinism is now clung to, as a philosophy rather than a limited methodological device, only by the defenders of a backward faith. For the alert and open thinker, scientism has collapsed. It is dead and gone.

II

The true prophet faces this loss of faith both in Christian ideology and in scientism. He relates his prophecy to our double heritage. He does not go back solely to the biblical faith of the early church or of the Reformers—as do false prophets—nor does he try to reconcile his faith with the false faith of scientism. The

true prophet of the living God relates his message to the total
heritage of his people, that is, to both Christian faith and to the
so-called scientific world view of modern man. He turns heritage
into history. He reconstructs heritage by appropriating it creatively. True history is always planted in heritage and also watered
there by the prophets of God's living history.

What are the false prophets of today saying? They are still
talking about God's mighty acts in Egypt and not about God's
deliverance of his people from present exile. There are four kinds
of false prophets. They are all related to our heritage, but not
creatively.

The fundamentalists, for our first example, are rejoicing in
the breakdown of scientism. That gives the primitive biblical
faith a chance once again. And to be sure, there is strong resur-
gence of traditionalistic Christianity. I see no chance for fundamentalism, however, unless we suffer a radical throwback in
civilization. It is both too immoral and too unintelligent. Scientism
may be collapsing, but thank God, as yet science remains.

On the other hand, those whose faith is scientism are rejoicing
in the collapse of Christian ideology. They are the fundamentalists of the so-called scientific world view. They practice their
occultism at the holy shrine of evolution, still believing that
science and education in the hands of enlightened man can change
the course of history and fulfill humanity. Their ranks are fast
thinning, but such false prophecy still sounds, especially from
duped academicians who have long ago forfeited their critical
reason for man-centered faith.

For a third example, we still have Barthian confessionalism,
by whatever name. This faith accepts God's revelation in Christ,
through the Bible and the church, for what it is, and secular
knowledge at its own estimate. It is a two-kinds-of-truth theory,
reviving the Middle Ages in our midst. Such separation can serve
the interests of both the church and educational institutions, but
it can never heal man's inner split between faith and knowledge,
nor does it ever let the full power of religious truth come to bear
on man's general knowledge. Nor is man's understanding of God
transformed by his fuller knowledge. As a *modus vivendi* such

confessionalism may play a temporary role, but it is evasion. It is false prophecy. These prophets have not stood in God's council; they still speak of God's mighty acts in Egypt in the past, not of God's rescuing his exiled people in the north country of today. The fourth kind of false prophet denies the reality of the very God who acts in history. For these prophets the personal God, the Spirit, the God of history is anthropomorphism. They dismiss faith in the Ultimate Concern and exchange it for religion as man's ultimate concern. Whereas the Barthian confessionalists may be thought of as sophisticated fundamentalists, these prophets of the Bultmann-Tillich school are really sophisticated religious modernists. Religion becomes a dimension of depth or man's authentic existence when opened to the stream of reality. Thus they have no council of God at all in which to stand, and they never expect God to deliver anyone from the exile of the north countries. Theirs is a fascinating response to both the Christian and the scientific heritages, but their prophecy is impotent in the face of our drastic and dire situation.

Man's religion has now come of age, says Bonhoeffer; a man no longer needs the hypothesis of God. I agree. The God of the hypothesis man can do without, but he needs desperately faith in and knowledge of the God who is, who acts, who holds the world in the hollow of his hand. Only those who have stood in his council can now prophesy. Only he can lead us from our present north countries into a new land, a new era.

III

The true prophet, who has stood in the council of God and who knows that God stands ready to deliver his people from the present exile in the north countries, must not only come to effective terms with our total heritage, appropriating it into living history; he must offer the world hope. What hope is there?

My abiding and growing conviction is that we can accept creatively what should be our two main heritages, the Christian faith and science (not the false heritages of Christian traditionalism and scientism), and still go creatively and fulfillingly beyond both by centering on a governing model, drawn from the Christian faith, yet exhaustlessly capable of expressing and appropriating all truth.

This model is the kind of life Jesus was and taught—the open, trusting, accepting love; the inclusive, creative concern through which we best see God. God is the Ultimate Concern seen in the suffering of the cross of Christ, but also in his creative teaching and healing. This concern is unconditional and eternal, yet immediately available and relevant to all life. This model fulfills life's deepest demand for freedom within the boundedness of our situation, and creates genuine self-being within a community of common concern. It is as personal as each person and ,yet as worldwide as the air and as long as the lastingness of eternal love. It is as intimate as your most private thoughts and decisions and yet as public as all our social, political, racial, and international problems. Through trust in God such concern can not only dissolve the barriers of fear's hate and alienation but also build the bridges of understanding and cooperation which alone can lead to new lives and a new age.

No amount of study or discussion will capture this model. It comes only to the trusting and concerned life, as we let ourselves go beyond the drives of desire and pushings of duty. Perhaps it comes to us best within our own lives through symbols that lay hold of our deepest heritage and yet challenge present history with hope.

I remember one day in Marburg, Germany, when for weeks I had been reading German theology, hoping for new light. I read and read but remained empty and disturbed at what seemed to me the sterility of the contemporary scene. Then I visited Saint Elisabeth's Church, that historic Hanseatic cathedral church of early Gothic purity, built in honor of her who became peculiarly instrumental in the establishing of Christian hospitals. As I went into one of the small chapels I saw there a two-level sarcophagus. On top reclined a splendidly dressed Teutonic knight, decked out in the full glory of his most festive regalia. Here was the ideal, and yet also once the actual, earthly splendor of man at his best. But underneath and as if within the sarcophagus was a jarring contrast. According to the instructions of the knight himself in the full heyday of his glory, he had been depicted on a lower level within the sarcophagus as a rotting corpse. The sunken, decaying body was overrun and being consumed by snakes and evil-looking toads. The two levels of this sarcophagus smote my weary and disappointed self with the vanity of life. No matter how high the glory there is always the same end of the story: decay and rot. Such is man's lot!

But as I turned, weary and depressed, into the main sanctuary with its high Gothic sweep my eyes fell on an old crucifix on one wall at the front of the nave—simple but crudely strong and utterly realistic. As I gazed at it, still filled with the thoughts of the vanity of life suggested by the sarcophagus in the anteroom I had just left, I suddenly was seized not by the vanity but by the meaning of life. The suffering heart of God ached within my own life. Somehow my search and disappointment were no longer merely personal but cosmic in dimension. Here was an authentic metaphysical experience. The crudely suggestive symbol of a life broken in concern for the world made faith live in me as no reading of books ever could. Here was meaning too deep for all rational expressions; yet I knew that it was the fullest answer to the mystery of life.

We face corruption and possible world collision. Personal and global life stand in danger of death, decay, and destruction. The prophets and preachers of today run though they are not sent; they prophesy though they have never stood in the council of the Lord. They learn from each other and spin out fancies to be admired. Therefore they speak of God's mighty deeds in the past. They proclaim God's great deliverance from Egypt. (For us that means in biblical times and in the times of the Reformation.) But they never face today with the full judgment of "repent or perish." They do not *know* the God who alone can save from the present exile of spiritual confusion and threatened destruction; they *have* no god to deliver them from the north country where we have now been driven.

But there are prophets who know the living God and who stand in his councils. They accept the heritage of our Christian tradition and of science, turning both into creative history lighted by hope. They no longer say that our hope is in

the Lord of Christian ideology or of scientism. Nor do they intend
to stay in the present exile of post-Christian nihilism and despair. They refuse to settle down in meaninglessness as though
it fed a hungry world with meaning. Rather their help is in the
name of the Lord who can deliver them from scattered confusion and emptiness in the present exile into their true homeland of both critical and creative reason.

The true prophets speak with integrity and power through
trust in God. They have stood in God's council; therefore they
will say, "As the Lord lives who helped the founding fathers
of our country, and who even delivered us from worldwide
destruction in the Cuban crisis." The true prophet will say, "As
the Lord lives who will usher in his new age, here, now, and
to the ends of the earth. As the Lord lives who will deliver
us from our present exile of nihilism and despair into our true
homeland of righteousness, truth, and creative concern, preg-
nant with expectancy and rich with new birth."

2.

A Future and a Hope

*I know the plans I have for you, says the Lord,
plans for welfare and not for evil, to give you a
future and a hope.* Jeremiah 29:11.

OUR CIVILIZATION can go one of two ways: toward growth or
toward decay. Our world can go one of two ways: toward newness of life or toward destruction. The decisive difference can
be made by the few who have been born into God's new age
for human history. Jeremiah once proposed this theme to the
faithful remnant of God's people.

We face times that are out of joint, and dread destruction
hangs over us. How can we arrogate to ourselves the right to a
text like this: "plans for welfare and not for evil, a future and
a hope"? Jeremiah faced worse times. His civilization had collapsed; his people had been taken captive; as a nation they
were no more. Humanly speaking, all hope was over. To these
exiles Jeremiah writes that God will give them a future and a
hope. But on God's own conditions. Can we with our civilization still standing, however much threatened and corroded,
appropriate rightfully for ourselves in faith the promises of God
for a future and a hope? Consider the conditions.

There is no future, claims Jeremiah, apart from the past. We
have to start where we are and act accordingly. There were
false prophets giving the people false hope. They assured the

19

people that God would restore their fortunes almost immediately. They told the people what they wanted to hear, that
God promised them a bright future forthwith. The future was
the gift of God's grace with little need to account for their
sins of the past that had led them into exile. Against such
false hopes and such an unrealistic future Jeremiah set his
face hard as flint. False hopes only deceive and disappoint. We
live in an age that is mostly hopeless because it is sick and
tired of false hopes. Jeremiah understood that the people had to
undergo their period of punishment; they had to be not only
reoriented and remotivated but reconstituted. No future or hope
would come, apart from an honest facing up to the past.

I

How can the future ever come to be different apart from our
dealing adequately with the past? We are our past. We cannot
get away from ourselves. We have made our bed, says popular
wisdom, and we must lie in it. Year after year I point out to
my students that there is no "was-ness" of the past, but only an
"is-ness." The past *was* but it never *is*. Only the "is-ness" of the
past remains. Yesterday was but never is. What remains of it is
part of today. Therefore life is utterly serious. In the East the
people dread the wheel of existence, for they know that deed
has consequences which cannot be escaped. In the Book of
Wisdom (17:21) God's punishment of the wicked is to chain
them to themselves, to put upon them "the burden of their own
companionship." How terrible that judgment can be. The worse
the selves, the more dread the doom. Not even suicide gets us
away from self. Hamlet was afraid perchance he'd dream. The
rub is far worse; it is to face the reality of ourselves in the
light of God. We are our past and cannot ever escape ourselves.

What we have done for good and evil also persists in the
present. The past persists in the present as the consequences
of our sin, the objective side of our guilt, or as the fruit of the
Spirit. Therefore any adequate dealing with our past must in-
volve the basic reconstitution of ourselves and of our past deeds.

This honest facing of the past is what Jeremiah put down as a condition before he could promise that God would give the remnant of his people a future and a hope. What the false prophets promised to the eager hearing of the unrepentant was that God would forgive and overlook the past.

The past calls for two basic attitudes and actions: repentance for the evil and gratitude for the good. Such repentance as can adequately deal with the past must be in depth. Fear's repentance, attrition, merely seeks selfishly to avoid the consequences. For false prophets that kind of repentance will do, but not for God. Duty's repentance can accept the consequences as just and set out to repair broken lives and a broken order. Duty can encourage reform—finding form again instead of the formlessness and the anarchy of evil—but only love's repentance can touch the inner self to turn it inside out toward God and others. Only contrition, the contrite heart, can find the full repentance that changes the self and sets out to remake the outside world.

God does forgive our sins freely. He even forgets them. Jeremiah says even that God remembers them no more (Jer. 31:34). He throws our sin behind his back (Isa. 38:17). God is ever willing to restore personal relationships when we are truly ready to renounce our evil past, particularly the evil past that we are. All our past that persists, that is actual, is in us now or outside us now in the form of the consequences of our deeds. When God forgives he does so at once. He does not wait for us to become right or to make things right. He receives us fully and freely. He never again holds our sins against us. They are forgiven as far as our lives are concerned; they are no more. They are thrown into the unreality of the canceled past. We are our past, but when we become new creatures in the present we let God erase the past that we were. How great and real is the Christian gospel of the forgiveness of sin.

But God never forgives or merely forgets the consequences. They have first to be faced up to and worked off in human history. I believe that the Roman Catholic insistence on doing penance is fundamentally right. If only the directives were more relevant to the actual putting things right in the objective order. No number of Hail Mary's will do that! Forgiveness involves both our becoming personally right with God and our becoming willing to set things right because we are motivated by the gratitude and love which always are part of true forgiveness. We are living in a world now where payment must be made. The innocent must pay the most if they know the innocence of forgiving and concerned love. Lincoln had few illusions. The lash of the whip brought on the strike of the sword. If we are to await God's new age it can come only on God's condition— our being forgiven and thus remotivated as well as redirected to take on the burdens and sufferings of the world. Only thus shall we face the past realistically, within the will of God.

Yet the past calls equally much for gratitude for the good. Only the sensitive spirit can be genuinely grateful. Only the lover can feel thanksgiving in full. We are indebted to all within the common web of life. Paul knew his debt to Jew and Greek, slave and free (Rom. 1:14). How should we enumerate the debts we owe today? Can we? What we are and have come out of a long past. We have received a priceless heritage of good which we mostly take for granted, an inheritance bought with untold love and care, labor and suffering, anguish and hope. As we celebrate our anniversaries do we authentically face our past with gratitude?

Especially are we thankful for the faithful few who have made possible what we are and have? Are you thankful for the small number who have made your life not only tolerable, but touched at times with the gentle breezes of heaven? Recall that Jeremiah wrote to a people who not only had sinned enough to perish, but who had produced those spiritual giants, the great prophets who wrote the morally majestic books of the Bible called after them. The worst times often call out the best people. We live through most trying times. Shall we only either accept or denounce our false prophets? Shall we not now rather also accept our good past with deep gratitude? Shall we not learn to recognize, to own and to heed the true prophets of today, of our relevant past, even as it is being made and as it is slipping away from us?

The honest, open spirit always repents of the evil past but accepts and owns its good with gratitude. With Jeremiah I now

call us to face our own past realistically, honestly before God.
For only so can we ever find the future we seek. First we must
deal adequately with the past—and we can, for God was in the
past, and underneath *were* the everlasting arms, and God can
therefore give us a future and a hope. Such are his promises:
"I have plans for welfare and not for evil, to give you a future
and a hope."

II

God's future and hope, however, always center in the present.
The past persists in the present as the present. We are our
past. We become our choices. But the past persists in the present, not as a dead lump, but as the living opportunity for the
future. Because we remake our past by the living of the present we can make a future out of our past. No present is merely
reliving the past, but it can be reduced almost to it if we concentrate on memory. Rather, as Kierkegaard writes, we must live
the past forward. We must repeat the past not by rote but
creatively, by the changing of it. Every present by the redoing
of the living past creates a new past for us. We change the past
in the present by turning it into the future. Hope is the living
of the past in the present as expectant faith.

We should accept the return of the past in the present with
no less realism than the Hindus who believe in karma, in deed
and consequence as the law of life. They know that every past
must be met in some present. We cannot handle all of it in
any present, hence different forms of karma; but we cannot ever
escape what we have done, for we are our choices. Therefore
we must accept the present realistically. We must have as much
realism as they, but I believe that because we have seen the
glory of God in the face of Jesus Christ we can have less fear
of the wheel of existence and more hope. Because we know
that God is faithful love, we believe that he will give us a future
and a hope.

Jeremiah asked the people to face the seriousness of their
past and to be willing to accept seventy years, if the account
is precise, of remedial living in exile. The false prophets, how-

ever, thought two years quite enough to redo the past. By
faith all things can be different since any redoing of the present involves the reconstituting of the past, but the use we make
of the present under God is decisive for the future. History is
flexible to faith. According to your faith it shall be done unto
you. Faith is trust; love is concern; but hope is expectation,
the actual looking for faith's concern to be realized.

If it is, we must commit ourselves to the constructive change
of our situation. That is what the present is for, as far as the
evil of life is concerned. To be sure, fundamentally we must
live in God, rest in God, accept and enjoy his love in every
present. Otherwise we become do-gooders and not men who
bring depth of change through height of hope. To accept the
status quo is to become guilty of original sin. We accept the
real, the good, and therefore we must reject the evil and bring
in reform. Reform is a strong, positive word, not the radical
rejection of the present but the rejection of the vague or false
form and the strengthening and improving of the true form of
life.

Today that means nothing less than beginning a new quality
of life that can be decisive for all history. We need now to
usher in concretely the new age of the universal man. God's
new age is the age of the universal faith. We must grow up as
men into the whole purpose of God. We must be willing to
experience true maturation. Call it Christian; call it real; call it
right; call it timely; call it the faith for one world; call it the
church of the Living God. The result is the same. God wants men
and women to live in a new universal spirit beyond family, beyond local loyalty, beyond nation, beyond race, beyond religion. All these have their necessary and good local expressions.
We must honor, enjoy, and serve these, for we human beings
are by circumstance local and limited. But we are all God's
children capable of participation in his universal life. Now is
the time to live this dimension.

We cannot do so by mere thought; we cannot do so by mere
will; we cannot do so within feelings alone; not even imagination will do, however sensitive and vast. We can do so only in
God who is the universal reality. Well has Teilhard de Chardin

pointed out in *The Phenomenon of Man* * that the scope of every atom in one of its aspects is the whole universe. We can be universal men and women in our very spirit, if we become rightly related to God. Teilhard sees that the decisive call for the future now comes in the form of our accepting, beyond mere thought, duty, or imagination, our full potential relation to God whereby we become under and with him the very remakers of history. In this present will you accept God's promise to give you a future and a hope, a constructive history in lives far different, qualitatively new, which alone can bear us into this new age? Will you accept the seventy years, symbolically speaking, of God's remaking us to return us from exile?

The call then is to our becoming remade in our very being. We must *be* God's will. We must release God's universal Spirit as the spiritual power for the remaking of human history and for the reconstituting of the new world. Saying and doing have their place; there is no vibrant or significant being that does not reveal itself in saying and doing. But what we must have now are people open, fully open, to God's universal Spirit, who live it naturally and constantly, like breathing and walking.

I know that God is in the present; underneath *are* the everlasting arms; therefore God will give us a future and a hope. We are our past, but we make our future in the present. God has all the resources ready and will give the needed guidance as we work toward his future. Will you know for yourselves that underneath are the everlasting arms and God will give us a future and a hope?

III

Jeremiah was God's true prophet. The false prophets saw their two years go by with the people still in exile. Theirs were false promises. But Jeremiah's prediction came true. After seventy years the exiles did return. They came back to their own land in God's good time. Seventy years in this instance surely stand symbolically for God's right time. There is no other time for the fulfillment of prophecy.

* New York: Harper & Row, 1959.

What is God's good time now? When will come our future and
our hope? All depends upon our response. Will we face the
past both in repentance and gratitude? Will we be realistic
about the way we meet the past in the present? Will we commit ourselves to constructive change? Above all, do we dare to
open our very beings unconditionally to God's concern for the
world? Will we dare to incarnate the Spirit?

The future comes today. It never comes as future. As future
it is always coming and never arriving. It is always on the way
but never the way we walk. The future comes as God's new
today in accordance with its own yesterday, which is now our
today. As such it comes as surely as the promises of God.

My hobby of gardening illustrates this point. All of a sudden
I may become aware of an ugly, uncultivated spot. My yesterday
of gardening stares me in the face today. But I repent my ill-
spent past and commit myself to constructive change. I prepare
the soil, I seed, I water, and I wait. Then some tomorrow will
be that day's today, and in it I see my better past. The past
that is then the present is my joy, the glory of the garden. What
a temptation, then, to focus merely on the past neglect, yet to
be remedied, or on some future yet to come. Sometimes I am
too busy to do more than pick off dead flowers and watch for
new buds instead of truly enjoying God's great gift of present
beauty. Tomorrow comes in gardening, but it comes as some new
today.

God's tomorrow will come for us all. What will it be like for
us? Will we return with joy and singing or shall we be carried
into exile, even destruction? The ten tribes did disappear. The
northern nation was destroyed. Israel perished. Judah had a
remnant restored after penitential suffering. Will we now be
totally destroyed as mankind? Such perishing seems realism. We
deserve it. History exhibits peculiarly God's long-suffering, but
even that recognizes when the final limit of persistent refusal
of God's will is reached. Will our whole world end in the final
conflagration?

Or is there even by some unheard-of mercy a chance to turn
history's corner of humanity into God's new age, into an im-
proved, a repentant world? Is there still a chance to accept our

past and radically to reform it in our present today? History shows both God's long-suffering and human urgency. Today may be decisive. Our life, our faith may change human history if we dare to accept into our very being, thinking, willing, doing, feeling, the universal will of God unconditionally. My own life is focused on that possibility. I live in expectant faith, believing that others, many others, will dare to give their lives for God's new day with the world. Millions are now suffering what seems near death. Millions have been sacrificed in fruitless wars in this century. Why should not a few of us dare to be under orders in a new way, God's orders for his new day?

Ultimately, however, this world will pass away. If we blow it up, will all things be as though nothing had ever been? To believe that is to be intellectually irresponsible. God's time is eternity. Our lives begin in God and go to God. This life is the smallest segment of our responsible choosing. Life after death is no question to him who has come upon the truth, the meaning of existence. It is as sure as God is. We need a radically larger understanding of God and of his eternal purpose. God's fuller future and hope for us is not on earth but in his own time—eternity.

Eternity, however, is entered only through time. Here and in the eternal conditions beyond our understanding, we know the moral seriousness in our choosing before God. Finally we have only two choices: to keep on being pursued in fear and misery by the Hound of Heaven, making our own bed in hell, or to accept the Everlasting Mercy of full freedom and fulfillment within the will of God. We can either flee from ourselves and from God, or we can find ourselves in finding the Love that will not let us go. Therefore to choose to become universal men and women now is to choose to enter into the reality of the gospel. We can do so only by God's grace and presence. For those who know what that means, even only as a foretaste, there is reality in God's promise that he will give us a future and a hope.

God's great today is awaiting us. His future knocks at the door of our lives. The gospel can give us,˙I believe, even yet the chance to repent and to live out the consequences of the past into some better future even in this life. Can we become sufficiently serious for such a choice? Or shall we let the Hound of Heaven bay at our heels as we flee God down the dark pathways of life's fear and needless pain in this world and in the world to come? The choice is ours.

God's promise is sure. He will be in the future. Underneath *will be* the everlasting arms, and he will give us, if we decide for it, a future and a hope.

3.

Externals, Internals, and Eternals

*I, Nebuchadnezzar, was at ease in my house and
prospering in my palace. I had a dream which
made me afraid; as I lay in bed the fancies and
the visions of my head alarmed me.* Daniel 4:4–5.

LOOKING AT THIS particular chapter in the Bible, Daniel 4, we
must remember that the Bible is written as a message from God
in times of need. A fundamental use of the Bible is to have God's
Word meet people's needs. In other words, this chapter is a simple message at a particular time. Most scholars say that this
chapter refers to Antiochus Epiphanes, the great tyrant in the
second century B.C., rather than to Daniel and Nebuchadnezzar
in the seventh. It doesn't make the slightest difference, because
the important thing is that God here has declared a message
that is real.

I

"I was at ease in my house and prospering in my palace,"
said the king; and never was Nebuchadnezzar's court more
flourishing. Then he went on, "I had a dream which made me
afraid." There seems to be no correlating of external situation
and internal satisfaction. A glorious morning can be sad, and
sometimes a dismal day externally will find us glad. Our inner
weather does not necessarily correspond with the outer weather.

A neurosurgeon at Children's Hospital in Boston stated that he thought it might be possible to change the body chemistry of the very young in such a way that we would not have these ups and downs. Thus one could adjust the emotional climate permanently. If only the human situation were as simple as that! Perhaps the surgeon is right, but I have my doubts. God has put us purposely in the kind of situation which, by its very nature, has to do with the internal and the external situation.

As far as the external situation was concerned, Nebuchadnezzar was well off. He says that never was his court more flourishing and he himself more at ease. His spirits were high, his health was good.

I talked with a missionary on leave from South Africa, a dedicated and competent man who had been one of my students. He was looking forward to going back, when he learned that he had cancer of the liver and perhaps six months to live. He told me, "You've no idea how I have sinned in always taking my health for granted. I've never been sick and I've never even thought about it, and here suddenly I confront this situation." Nebuchadnezzar apparently didn't have a health problem, for he "was at ease."

Furthermore, he had no family problems. I hardly need to mention how many people have family problems. Some people even think, as I read not long ago, that if a person says he has no family problems, he is neurotic! If a woman refers to her husband as a slob, said the article, she tends to be normal, but if she says that he is thoughtful and considerate, you had better examine her inner motivations! I can testify, however, to the fact that there are such things as warm, genuine families where the members support each other not only in spirit, but in all their relationships. Nebuchadnezzar had no family problems or he wouldn't have been at ease.

Nor was he at war. He was prospering in his palace. He had everything he wanted. He had not only health, but wealth, all the fancy foods, all the women he wanted, he could travel anywhere he wanted, he could have anything. He had it made!

Sometimes the external things look so right to others—but not right to ourselves. One day I woke up and learned that someone at the seminary where I taught had done something against me that I thought was pretty mean. Inwardly I was rather provoked about it. I huffed and puffed around the house and I went up to school in this kind of spirit. Why had this person done this thing? The president called me in and said, "Now, Nels, I want you to bear with some people who don't always understand. You ought to do that, because you have everything." Here I was fussing about externals, while others looking at me felt that I "had everything." When I began to think about it, I tended to agree. It isn't a question necessarily of how we look at the externals, but what the externals actually are. So Nebuchadnezzar had everything.

II

Just then, in the midst of ease and prosperity, he had a dream that made him afraid. Although he had all the externals, a dream suddenly alarmed him. This is the century when we are learning about dreams. All of us have read or heard of Jung and Freud and Adler. We know dreams, we know about the internal workings of the subconscious; and these dreams can be quite vivid.

I remember my professor of theology many years ago telling of his son who dreamed that he and his sister were coming out of an old-fashioned drug store when the wooden Indian outside came to life and began chasing them. The next morning at the breakfast table the boy was telling the family about this dream. His little sister got more and more excited and finally blurted out, "Then what happened? Then what happened?" "You tell it yourself," her brother said in disgust. "You were there, weren't you?"

Dreams can indeed be vivid. We also know that even though the externals may seemingly be all right, people suddenly have breakdowns. We all know of people who seem to "have everything," to be the belle of the ball, so to speak, who suddenly "drop out" or enter a convent or perhaps even commit suicide. They flee the world because even though everything external seems to be right, there is something internal that is not satisfying them. Not only can people have conflicts, but they can repress conflicts in such a way that when things seem to be all very well, something else is working deeply within. Suddenly, even in the most secure situation, there can come a dream that makes people afraid and begins to give them fancies that alarm them, even as these fancies alarmed Nebuchadnezzar.

In his dream Nebuchadnezzar saw a great tree reaching up to heaven. Like everyone in those days, he thought of the earth as flat, vaulted over by heaven. The tree reached all the way up to heaven, and the flat earth was surrounded by oceans. People from all around could see this tree. They sat under it, they received their fruit from it, and they received their shade from it. This tree was their sustenance and their health. They rejoiced in it. Then suddenly there came a voice from heaven which said, "Hew down the tree, strip it, and leave only the stump." Nebuchadnezzar could not understand the dream.

We all have had interesting dreams which we wish we could understand. I know a theologian who took the drug LSD. This drug commonly creates an experience in which one sees himself die. He goes through the hell of seeing himself as he really is. My friend described vividly his dream in which he saw a great pagoda and a tremendous idol which was never satisfied. As he kept on offering more gifts, the idol wanted more and more. Then to the man's horror he realized that he was himself the idol, and the gifts that he was trying to give were his Ph.D., his books, his fame, and all the things he was seeking. But no matter how much he received from the world, he was just as dissatisfied, because he wanted more and more and more.

My theologian friend said, in effect, "I thought I had it made. I had everything external. It went well with me, but now I can't feel that way any more. I know that from within I am a selfish person concerned with self-promotion and self-protection. What I am interested in is really not God. I am not really interested in what is going to happen to my people. I am interested primarily in myself."

I would certainly not recommend that anyone try this dangerous drug. My point is that this theologian discovered how he really felt and was astonished to learn that he was far from being as good as he thought he was.

III

Nebuchadnezzar needed to go beyond the externals and the internals to the eternals. This great monarch's dream meant that he had to be humbled. He had to lose his mind. He had to become like an animal and eat grass and suffer a mental breakdown for seven years until he came to accept God, "till you know that the Most High rules the kingdom of men, and gives it to whom he will." Only when he finally realized that God and God alone has the right way with men could he receive back his reason. Then, at last, Nebuchadnezzar could say, "My reason returned to me; and for the glory of my kingdom, my majesty and splendor returned to me. . . . and I was established in my kingdom, and still more greatness was added to me."

As human beings we share Nebuchadnezzar's problem. We need to understand ourselves in the light of reality, and God is reality. Nebuchadnezzar could not get this understanding from the false prophets; he got it from Daniel. But not even understanding was enough to help him.

I worked for several years with a group of psychiatrists and theologians in a discussion of our common problems. These psychiatrists admitted frankly that it is easier to get people to understand themselves than it is to lead them, after they understand themselves, to transfer this understanding into living a creative and confident life. Nebuchadnezzar understood himself when Daniel interpreted the dream; nevertheless he broke down, because he did not have the internal resources to open his life to God.

This is also true with us. I have come to believe that what we need in today's world more than anything else is a genuine understanding of who the living God is and what the living God wants. But more than that, we have to go beyond understanding to the kind of right relationship with God in which we give him not only glory (because he wants no glory) but also the acceptance of our lives as individuals and civilizations in terms of which we ourselves can become reconstituted and remotivated and recreated within, and civilization can itself become right.

I don't know how much you suffer. I don't know how much

you struggle with the world's problems. Have you really been struggling lately about the world's peace? Honestly, have you been suffering, have you been agonizing, have you been praying, have you been concerned that we stand now at a time when we might either go on to a new, constructive civilization or else destroy the whole world? Has this meant everything to you, or have you been concerned mostly with your work, your plans, and your personal problems while we have this pressing external situation?

The race problem confronts us. Never before in the history of our country, or perhaps the world, has the challenge of race come upon us so suddenly. Some of our responsible Christian leaders stand aside and do what they can, but there is more and more ambiguity in the situation. We know that there must be a new day and we are willing to do anything, but we are perplexed about what to do.

I was speaking with one of the civil rights leaders who was just out of jail on bail. This was before the assassination of Martin Luther King. He said that he did not think the black people were going to follow the nonviolent leadership of Martin Luther King. He felt that they were going on to violence and that we would not be able to solve the problem peacefully. The white people, he said, are not going to come across in time, and there is going to be bloodshed and a great deal of civil strife. His prophecy has been partly true. I have been agonizing about this and I have been asking how I can do my part. And I don't know.

I could go on to problem after problem. Here we are, facing God's world. Have we learned that we need to pay attention both to externals and to internals, but only in the light of the eternal? Have we learned this crucial and fundamental fact?

I was brought up in Sweden, and I have watched that country within a generation become almost a human paradise externally. There is no poverty in Sweden, no slums, no basic unemployment. There is no question of financial worry about hospitalization or medical care. Everybody gets a vacation, even a housewife, I have been told, with the children taken care of. Humanly speaking, here is a mature culture and an extremely well-ordered society. But the Swedish people have not thereby solved their fundamental problems. Not only has religion declined, with only some 2 to 9 percent, depending on estimates, supporting the churches, but there are also other internal problems—meaninglessness of life, juvenile delinquency, alcoholism. These are only a small part of the situation, however, and I must not exaggerate them, but they indicate that there is no solution of the world's problems in terms of mere externals, or else we would have solved them by this time.

We face externals and we must treat them intelligently and honestly and constructively. But I know that that is not going to cure our problems. We must also meet the internal problems. But even that is not itself enough, because man is not only living in the external world and the internal world. He lives in the eternal world. He lives in relation to God.

Many years ago my Model T Ford ran into a street car. Again and again I took it back to the mechanic to be repaired. He finally said, "You are a student; take my advice and sell the junk. You will never be able to run this car right because the chassis is out of alignment and something will always snap, something will always be wearing out."

The trouble with our civilization, the trouble with us, is that we are not right with God. Our "chassis" is not in alignment. When in humility, in repentance, in true reform we open up to the will of God, then shall come upon us such creative leadership and such inner power to cope with our external problems that God's new age shall become a reality, and we shall not destroy the world, we shall not suffer our children's children to bear the consequences of our continuing to sin against the light.

Externals may seem right, but when internals are wrong, both external and internal have to become right in the light of God's eternal Word. Then he will give us the joy of our salvation and the practical, realistic power to cope with all our problems; then men shall rise up and call us blessed, because in truth we are.

4.

Extremism Without Extremity

> *Let your eyes look directly forward. . . . Do not
> swerve to the right or to the left; turn your foot
> away from evil.* Proverbs 4:25, 27.

EXTREMISM IS NOW much in the news. The general opinion is that
extremism is evil and dangerous, leading to extremity. Man can
easily go off the deep end either on the right or on the left.
Extremism generally becomes equated with fanaticism, and fanaticism is both blind and deadly.

But there is an extremism without extremity. The Christian
faith enjoins full acceptance and engenders complete faithfulness. We cannot understand the heart of the Christian faith and
accept it with tentativeness or reservation. Thomas Kelly in *A
Testament of Devotion* * goes so far as to call the claims of Christ
totalitarian. Can there be Christian extremism that is extremism
without extremity?

Extremism is supposed to be exciting. I am going to recommend the most exciting extremism, not one that is at either
extremity, right or left, but the extremism that is at the extreme
center.

The Christian faith centers in God as Love, in the Holy Spirit as
the Truth, and in Christ as God's Love and Truth. Now when

---

* New York: Harper & Row, 1941.

Christian love, *agape*—God's universal, unconditional concern—is carried to its extreme, there can never be too much of it. Fanaticism is ruled out by the very nature of that love which focuses in the welfare of the other. That love, therefore, possesses an inborn self-corrective feedback system whereby the more genuinely it is expressed, the more it relates to the other person and to all others according to need. If the other person needs help, *agape* gives it. If the other needs to be left alone, he who lives *agape* provides the opportunity. If the situation of the other needs first of all to be studied, concern never substitutes intention for inquiry.

There can be lack of *agape*; there can be the name without the reality, for human sin and finitude exist; but there can never be too much genuine love, for God is Love. We are made for love, and we can be fulfilled only in love. Love seeks freedom and fulfillment for every man and for all men in all their relations—to God, to each other, and to nature.

The Christian extreme is thus extremism without extremity. It is freedom and fullness of life. It is creative adventure in daring concern. To such extremism we are called in three areas of life: (1) theology, or man's quest for ultimate meaningfulness; (2) community, or man's dimension as a social being as well as a self; and (3) selfhood, or man's need for maturity.

I

Christian theology is nearly ready to start out on the straight path in the extreme center. The adventures toward Christian truth already have become a lure to the spiritually sensitive and to the intellectually alert.

Theology deals with the central and most dependable meaning for life. All people live by meaning. All organize life's meaning for them into some pattern of life. To live is to choose meanings. To keep on living is to accumulate meanings. The main pattern of life is one's theology. It may be confused, contradictory, partial, inconsistent, but unless life breaks there is some pattern. All people have a theology. All live by faith. All walk an unknown and unproved way. The only difference is that some have a considered and others an unconsidered theology. Some can interpret the meaning of life, enjoy its adventure, employ its opportunities, and direct their steps toward a fulfilling destiny. Others either fail to know that they can do so or fail in the attempt.

Christian theology is life directed by and within the love of God toward open concern with and for others. It is the living of the truth in love. Therefore it swerves neither to the right nor to the left. Christian theology steers clear of both the reactionary right and the negative left. Such extremisms are misleading and unproductive. Rather, Christian theology directs its creative life toward the fresh findings at the extreme center; it works rewardingly at extremism without extremity.

The reactionary right in Christian theology shrinks before the problems and impotence of the modern age and cries for an imagined past. It always arrogates to itself the right to the term "orthodoxy," meaning by that the faith of our fathers, but fails to see that true orthodoxy is the moving straight forward toward the desired destination. So-called orthodoxy is always man's meanest and most dangerous heresy.

Not being open in spirit to the creative adventure of the forward march, the reactionary right idolatrizes the frozen past. It freezes the Bible into petrified pages and worships it as the Word of God instead of as the fresh, living speech of the God of the forward march. Instead of following the pillar of fire by night and the cooling cloud by day of the God of the onward march, the so-called orthodox sit motionless in front of static creeds. They extol authority, but they become authoritarian rather than authoritative. The reactionary right is not Christianity today but the backwardness and the tyranny of yesterday. To all those who are far away from the hazards of the creative adventure into the constructive gospel, I offer the biblical injunction: "Let your eyes look directly forward. Do not swerve to the right or to the left."

On the other side of the road to freedom and fulfillment in the gospel that speaks the truth in love is the negativity of the left. The radicals on the left repudiate the false past of a spurious orthodoxy. They identify the Christian faith with an unprogressive past and scorn it as static. They equate the Christian faith with unreconstructed dogma and claim to have outgrown it. In thus denouncing and renouncing the false past, they voice much that is good and needed. But they fail to move ahead positively toward the desired destination of the truth and the love in and from God that engender mature manhood and creative community. They never move forward toward basic fulfillment in freedom which is man's true goal.

Tillich and Bultmann, for example, veil the emptiness of their theology behind symbols and myths, but their theologies offer false breasts that cannot feed the child; and for the mature they provide only mouth-watering pictures of meat but not its substance. Against a false past they are gleaming highways; as pioneers toward the fulfilling future they are at best attractive side roads toward the eventual desert of man's ultimate spiritual starvation. Bishop Robinson, as a revolter against the past, lures us along at a rollicking pace; for the most part he is relevantly and importantly right, but his road leads straight across the road ahead at the creative center into the byways of leftist negation.

We who have started with full commitment to build for the future must take the way of extremism without extremity. We will want to pursue the creative road ahead of constructive Christian theology.

The Christian faith in its past formulation will not do. The love of God the Spirit, the Father of us all, has never been taken seriously at the center of Christian theology. The Christian faith has always been both diluted and distorted by some alien dualism. Throughout most of its history Christian theologians have tried to formulate it in terms of some substance philosophy, some understanding of what is ultimate in terms of being. But God is not being; God is Spirit. God is not substance; God is Love. God is not personality even, but personal Spirit.

My claim, and I know that it is well founded, is that the Christian faith as truth has never been developed from within its own categories. These categories go deeper and wider than the contrast between the Western stress on being and the Eastern stress on nonbeing; they are far more fundamental than the

difference between primary stress on being or on becoming.
The Christian faith is true. It must be freed from a diluted and
distorted past, from its suffocation within the reactionary right,
but also from the futility and fugitiveness of the negative left.
Both authoritarian dogmas of revelation and agnostic vacuum
must be left behind in spirit and in matter, in method and in
doctrine, in faith and in life.

My first pointer toward creative renewal is, then, the repudi-
ation of both the reactionary right—even when it claims to be
the historic center—and also the negative left no matter how
sophisticated and alluringly modern it may sound, in order to
turn with fresh courage and with creative vision to that true
center of the Christian faith, God as the personal Spirit who is
agape, for which and in which the new world is waiting to be
born.

II

If your eyes look directly forward and you swerve neither to
the right nor to the left, but keep your foot away from evil, you
will also develop genuine Christian community beyond religion,
beyond nation, beyond race, beyond class, in fact, beyond all
limiting ingroups even of family and friends. The Christian community is universal, open to all, motivated by God's unconditional
love, the total self-giving symbolized and summarized by the
Cross of Christ. In Christ can be no Christian or Jew, no communist or capitalist, no black or white, no educated or uneducated,
no distinguished or undistinguished, no rich or poor, certainly no
Roman Catholic or Protestant, let alone Baptist or Lutheran.
These labels belong outside the true temple, only in the court of
the Gentiles, to use biblical terminology, not in the holy of
holies.

In Christ all are one. In the Spirit there is unity. Christian
community is full freedom and faithfulness in fellowship built
on the kind of love first fully revealed and made effective as light
and life in Jesus Christ. This is Christian extremism for community. This is the extreme center of God's love for all. This is
extremism without extremity.

The reactionary right is far off-center in this realm. It stands for the Christian faith as monolithic revelation. It says all other religions are false and must make unconditional surrender.

For those on the reactionary right communism is totally wrong; they make no distinction between Marxist philosophy and the insistent rising of the people to freedom. They seldom recognize even those truths in Marxist philosophy which have been lifted right out of biblical eschatology—the basic pronouncements on property in the Acts of the Apostles, and the historic Christian labor theory of value—but label all of communism pagan and evil. Those who hold to the reactionary right are also seldom aware of the complete contradiction of Christianity and racial segregation; they are unaware that segregation spells sin in directly Christian terms.

The negative left is far off the road, too, but since it mostly attacks the reactionary right it could appear that it is calling for progress. But the road ahead is found only within the revealed truth—and the truth open for further constructive seeking. The negative left advocates that no religion is true, that all are relative, that each religion is best for its own people. Therefore the negative left is agnostic; its pluralism is based on man's ultimate ignorance. Its tolerance is the acceptance of no dependable direction. Instead of all the truth being revealed once for all within an authoritarian revelation, the negative left sponsors common seeking without ever finding ultimate truth.

Similarly the negative left imagines an internationalism without religious direction and motivation. Man cannot live without ultimates. "One world" in political need calls for one religion as its basis. The negative left knows little or nothing of the power of the Spirit to change the climate, to effect legislation, to constrain acceptance and creative ways of cooperation. Much can be accomplished by concerned pressure, but no political or social situation can be cured that way. The healing hand of God's Spirit has other approaches ready.

The extreme center of the Christian gospel, however—the good news that is true—offers God's universal, unconditional love in Christ which is forever the pure gift of God himself to man. God is beyond religion; therefore his sons must be so also. We live in a world of which God is the only creator, the maker of heaven and earth and of all men. But the world man makes is full of many religions and always will be, for religion is man's response to God.

The one religion is man's response to God's universal, unconditional love wherein the unity of the Spirit does not deny the diversity of gift, where the unity of the one Spirit of love and understanding does not deny the many ways that Spirit can engender rich differentiations of human community, even religiously. Extremism without extremity refuses both the dogmatism of the one and only true religion and the dogmatism of the many religions that are merely relative and pluralistic. We may have to give up historic developments as ultimate, even historic names, but the finality of faith remains—in Christ as God's universal, unconditional Love and in the Holy Spirit as the Spirit of Truth who shall lead us too into all truth.

Thus also, as we press ahead at the center of truth in faith and freedom, we shall get beyond both nationalism and romantic one-worldism. When there was no larger effective unit of law and order, the sovereign nation served God in this respect. Thus nationhood was part of natural law. But now the day of sovereign nations is obviously over, along with feudalism and colonialism. We live in a new day which must have world reign through world law and world sanctions. Either this, however achieved, or destruction.

We have to provide the faith that corresponds to our new situation. A spiritual and moral order must undergird and motivate this one world; it will affect race and class, yes, even the economic system. In all respects we shall need radical change. Yet this change must not be such as to ignore the differences in creation, whether of color, of ability, or of power. It is an insult to God to say that a Christian is color blind, meaning not even aware of race. Would one want to be color blind in the garden and to see all flowers alike? No! Exult in color and accept it as God's enrichment!

Similarly, we must recognize ability and reward it. And by all means let us understand what the technological revolution of our day requires, and not try to live economically in our paltry yesterdays. Release the whole productive market; distribute economic power and wealth according to both the common good and personal growth and satisfaction. Let us learn from every system how to achieve by God's grace maximum freedom with maximum security, maximum responsibility for all with maximum reward. The point is that the Christian faith, the extremism without extremity, has the formula for our straight walking toward the desired destination: *freedom and faithfulness in fellowship*. We should swerve neither to the right nor to the left in the implementing of this formula.

III

Extremism without extremity leads directly to the fulfilled person of Christian maturity or, to use biblical expressions, to the mature manhood which is the full measure of Christ for every man (Eph. 4:13). The love of God in Christ alone offers such full manhood. We see God in Christ; we see man in Christ. Christ is the true mediator between God and man because he is the straight road that God has made to himself—but a way that each person must himself walk in order to get there. Only unconditional, universal Love, austere, unsentimental, responsible, intelligent, passive and receiving, active and giving, open, creative and free, can ever satisfy the depths of man. Man is made for God and can never escape this primary fact. But he is so made for God that God will not have him unless he is willing to open his life fully and freely to all human beings. Only universal man is the true Christian person.

The right as well as the left reacts negatively to the gospel. The reactionary right of Christian anthropology divides Christ off from all men. He is God walking in a human body. This view is definitely docetic, denying Christ's full ordinary humanity. It is the heresy of one extremity, the deity without the humanity. It flees the truth of Incarnation, the full relevance of the Christ for mankind, by arrogating to its indubitably heretical position the name of orthodoxy. Perhaps nothing has done

more to nullify the Christian faith as an effective force in human
life and human history than this removal of Jesus from man
behind a false façade of specious orthodoxy.

In similar fashion the negative left has denied the deity of
Jesus, the historic reality of God's entering history in Jesus as
a unique historic event, fulfilling once and for all human history.
From now on what we do is to appropriate and to live that
fullness. From now on we are to make our own the fullness
that God has given us in Christ.

For the good of man and for the good of the future, however,
the Christian extreme—the extremism of the creative center
but not of either extremity—must understand and accept what
the genuine Christian gospel is, namely, that in Christ we see
the true nature of God and the true nature of man as unconditional, universal Love. Humanly speaking such a statement
is absurd. Man is in himself constitutionally and circumstan-
tially incapable of such love. So he is. But man is never true
man by himself. Man is himself only in right relation to God
and to all others, and to all nature as well. That relation is
defined normatively by Chalcedon, God in man, without di-
vision and without confusion, yet in one true historic personality. Jesus in his true relation to God was precisely also true
man. Only by understanding and accepting this relation shall
mankind be able to enter that new age which is now God's
call to human destiny.

If each person is potentially related to all in the spirit, what
we need is a new spirit. There are depths of spirit yet un-
tapped to remake life and to release unthought-of creativity and
fullness of genuine satisfaction of life. Our new atomic age must
be outmatched by the new age of mind and spirit, but above
all of spirit. We must work at this in full openness, expectation, and discipline with far more fervor and diligence than
did those who worked to beat Nazi Germany to the finding and
use of atomic power.

The power for the few to change the world will come through
faith, as we encounter the Holy Spirit in full openness and in
unequivocal expectation, and as we join the community of the
universal man, of complete concern, of the living God. We must

encounter God in prayer without ceasing; our whole lives must be universal within the will of God for the world. When we see that face of God, and when we accept that face of God, the Holy Spirit whom we have encountered will become our "within"; he will become our own lives. The Incarnate Word, that in Jesus began to make one world and to make of all one, will then have that same power in us. Thus the new mature manhood we need is the full measure of Christ in us by the presence of the Holy Spirit.

We need a new theology. We need a basic reorientation and remotivation of all our social, political, and economic life. We need their total redirection within the full power and understanding of the deeper realities of the Spirit. God is calling us to creative adventure. The world waits for the new mind and the new spirit. At its center the Christian faith has the answer. It is up to us to receive it. To do so we must swerve neither to the reactionary right nor to the negative left. We must keep in the center of the road of God's creative love. We must not let our foot turn away to evil but keep our eyes looking directly forward.

5.

From the Sacred to the Secular

Their leaves will not wither nor their fruit fail, but they will bear fresh fruit every month, because the water for them flows from the sanctuary. Ezekiel 47:12.

FRUIT HAS ALWAYS been one of mankind's delights. Indeed, the world almost worships fertility. What could be more interesting to us than creativity? Sometimes I get fascinated wondering what caused the creative ages of civilization. Why should there have been such a tremendous sixth century B.C. during which, in different parts of the world, the great religions began to be born? Why? Sunspots? Why should there have been the great culture of sixth- and fifth-century Greece? Why should the Christian era have come when it did? What caused the Renaissance? What makes any age creative? How do we set about, if we can, to make our own a creative age?

In South Dakota one time I found a small church in a small city which had in it the national president of the young people's society of the whole denomination, the president of the state conference, the president of the county conference, and the president of the city conference. It was only a little church, but the members said matter-of-factly, "We keep doing this." There was a little church in, I think, Waycross, Georgia, that long ago in a short span of time brought forth a crop of outstanding people in different lines—in the Senate, in literature, and in other fields.

What makes some people and some churches and some places so creative? There are homes, there are people, there are places and groups that, wherever they touch, bring forth wells of healing, wells of creativity.

I

Our text says that fresh fruit will be borne every month—that is, dependably—because the water flows from the sanctuary. We are living now in an age that has little use for the sanctuary. Our age worships secularism. If you want to be in style today, you run down the church. If you want to be "with it," you call yourself post-Christian or postreligious. Or you sagely quote Bonhoeffer to the effect that God has set us free in Jesus Christ even from himself, set us free from religion, set us free because the world has come of age and we no longer need the hypothesis of God. Yes, this is the seal of our age. Churches and religion are outdated. Even Christianity is icky business—somehow or other it is weird and wrong and uncomfortable. We must *out* from the church, we must *out* from religion, we must *out* from the sanctuary into the world, because it is in the world we find God, and not in the sanctuary.

Bishop Robinson in *Honest to God* * says that when he was a theological student he didn't dare to admit that prayer meant nothing to him and that worship meant very little. But now that he has read some of the modern theologians who say that we don't need to believe any of that kind of stuff any more, he is quite relieved. He can be "honest to God." Therefore he accepts religion as referring to the secular world. The mystical, the moral, the spiritual belong to the church's reality, which itself is part of the secular world. Religion in the old sense is sham.

II

But this doesn't jibe with our text. The text says that there can be dependable fruit from a dependable source because

* Philadelphia: The Westminster Press, 1963.

the water flows from the sanctuary. Elton Trueblood once stated that we live in a cut-flower civilization, in a rootless age. We are enjoying the fruit while denying the roots. But we shall not again produce real fruit until we are willing to acknowledge and be rightly related to the roots. It is easy to eat the fruit while we have it, but it is another thing to produce it.

Culture historically is the child of religion. If we read the histories of science, such as those of George A. Sarton and Alfred North Whitehead, we find that it was religion that prepared a kind of view of reality, a view of the universe in terms of which man's cultural activities found their inception and their motivation. For instance, in Marburg, Germany, one sees the beginning of Christian hospitals in the work of Saint Elisabeth, who gave of herself completely because of her Christian concern. Her caring for the sick led to more and more of this kind of work.

God is the source of significance, and he is the center of creativity. Every age that wants truly to become creative, every person who genuinely wants to find the fullest fulfillment of his life and have his fruit remain—or as the more poetic version of the Bible says, "abide" *—must be rightly related to the Source. Worship is the right relation with God that finds access to the fruit of the spirit.

Probably one reason that the Jewish people have maintained their identity so long and so well is that they have taken Ezekiel's word. They have put the sanctuary in front of the house. The Jewish family traditionally makes religion a center, and because of this abiding loyalty Judaism has maintained itself over the centuries. But the sanctuary itself is no true sanctuary when it stands isolated and self-concerned and removed from the world. The only true sanctuary of God is the one that by its very nature lives in the world, is concerned for the world, relates itself to the world, becomes involved in the world. When a church is interested mainly in itself and in maintaining its own organization, raising its own budget, padding its own statistics, that church dies spiritually. When a church

* John 15:16, KJV.

opens itself in sacrificial, true, genuine concern for the world, this church receives from that Source of significance and that spring of creativity the life that can grow and build itself up in love.

What a strange and wonderful vision Ezekiel had! The creatures he saw had wings on all sides (Ezek. 1). We might say that God's help could come at any time or in any direction, for the wheels went in all directions. Wherever there was need, there was God. In other words, God's sanctuary is not one that sits up on high and to which people must somehow arduously find their way. The sanctuary is God's constant concern—God who knows, cares, and loves, who is more willing to come to us than we to the sanctuary. And insofar as we accept that sanctuary, that sanctuary goes into our lives and we go out to others —because now we have received the wings on all sides, and we have the wheels on all sides, and we relate ourselves to every place there is need. This is the picture: not the world *or* the sanctuary, but the sanctuary in the midst of the world, thereby becoming involved, thereby becoming creative, because the sanctuary is the sanctuary of God's concern.

How did the present movement in America to change the racial situation come to be? It came out of many sources and out of much praying and believing, but the one who triggered it was Martin Luther King, Jr. How did Martin Luther King begin? He began with the theology of love, of *agape*. He began with the theology of God's complete concern. In India he learned the method of applying it, but *agape* was his moving spirit. Martin Luther King maintained that if we get away from the spirit of caring completely and utterly for *all* people, we are going to lose the power to change race relations. Winning civil rights through legislation is a hollow victory without acceptance on the part of all people.

When Martin Luther King's home in Montgomery was bombed, a throng of a thousand angry black men and women quickly assembled. Threats of violence quivered in the air. But King stood on the bombed porch and raised his arms for silence. In his rich preacher's voice he ordered the crowd not to panic, to do away with their weapons, to abandon the idea of trying to get even through violence. He went on to say, as William Robert Miller movingly relates in his biography, " 'We must love our white brothers no matter what they do to us. We must make them know that we love them. Jesus still cries out in words that echo across the centuries: "Love your enemies: bless them that curse you; pray for them that despitefully use you." This is what we must live by. We must meet hate with love.' " * And the crowd drifted quietly away.

This is the Christian spirit. Here is fruit that is going out through all the land and throughout the world, fruit that is born from the water flowing from the sanctuary. This is the true motivation. This is the only way we shall ever really and fundamentally change the world, because we shall change both people and conditions. This is the way God works.

Roger Babson was surely right when he investigated the question of why certain Americans had become successful, and discovered, in going through *Who's Who,* that a large proportion of these people had come from homes where they had kept the Sabbath. A generation or two ago family worship was prevalent. Somehow or other a tremendous creativity came from these homes. I can witness to the fact that it is the dedicated homes that turn out creativity. (Sometimes there are exceptions, of course, because God has given us freedom, even to revolt.) But the fundamental drive, the fundamental motivation, the fundamental creativity is there.

The rightness of race, the rightness of place, the rightness of condition flows from the sanctuary. Right relation to God produces fruit dependably. Religion begins in mysticism or prayer and ends in politics. The religion that is not centered in this ultimate relationship of worship is not right, and the religion that does not carry through until it touches every part of life is not true. Religion includes all human affairs. The cure for bad religion is good religion, not no religion. Warren Wagar, the author of *The City of Man,* writes his personal conclusion in a

* William Robert Miller, *Martin Luther King, Jr.: His Life, Martyrdom and Meaning for the World* (New York: Weybright and Talley, 1968), p. 46.

letter in 1968 to the effect that man will always be a faith-producing and faith-bearing creature.

III

Religion is an inescapable reality. The question is not getting away from religion, being "postreligious," but seeing that the Christian faith at its center is the truth for mankind. The problem is not to get away from either the Christian faith or religion in general, but so to understand the very center of religious reality and the meaning of the Christian faith, that in this unconditional love of God we begin to understand nature, history, and human life. When our church is caught by the vision and motivated by the power, it will again become that central sanctuary, the source that enables us to keep bearing creative fruit, touching others with this creative reality. *The Spirit is the Source of significance;* the sanctuary is the well of creativity.

I am very fond of gardening. Growing flowers is my hobby. Anybody who grows petunias knows that you have to keep picking off the dead blossoms. That little petunia is determined to set seed; you have to let it keep constantly creative if you are going to keep it blossoming. I read an account of scientists experimentally removing a piece of the heart from a chicken. They kept it running for years. If it had remained in the chicken it would have died long ago,* because it would have fulfilled its purpose. But it continued to tick on because it didn't know that its purpose had been fulfilled!

The great biochemist Charles S. Sherrington, in *Man on His Nature,*‡ says there is no reason at all in terms of biochemistry why we should ever die. The only reason we grow old and die is that we seem to have fulfilled our purpose, from one point of view. But no one is any older and no one is any less alive than the purpose which motivates his life. It is possible at any age or at any time, from youth to age, to be so filled with the creativity

* Charles S. Sherrington, *Man on His Nature,* 2nd ed. (Cambridge: Cambridge University Press, 1953), p. 76.
‡ Ibid.

of God's presence that when we touch our grandchildren (or when they touch us) water flows dependably from the sanctuary.

No one is too young or too old to be touched by a purpose, touched by a vision, touched by a reality. Anyone may become a changed and different person. Life becomes different when the water truly flows from the sanctuary. It can touch any person at any time and make that person creative and bear fruit, become meaningfully alive, rich with the power and reality of the gospel.

I am not ashamed of the gospel. The only things I am ashamed of are all the words, the shibboleths, all the easy talk, all the sham that surrounds religion. That I am ashamed of. I want more and more—I want us all more and more—to get away from the externals and superficials and enter into the reality of God's presence, so that we ourselves may let God give us wings on all sides and wheels on all sides.

"Come ye to the fountain and drink without money." * You can't pay for the gospel. When everything is said and done, you can pay for the availability of it, in one sense, but the gospel is free. The gospel is opening our native selves to the purpose for which God made us. "Come ye to the fountain, drink without money," without cost, or let us paraphrase it, "Come to my orchard and eat fruit." The fruit of the Spirit will grow in our lives, because we will have that dependable Source for creativity that flows from the sanctuary. Because the water that sustains our life flows from the sanctuary, we will bless the world by our presence.

* Isa. 55:1; Rev. 21:6; 22:17.

6.

Making Prayer Effective

*Far be it from me that I should sin against the
Lord by ceasing to pray for you.* 1 Samuel 12:23.

A FEW YEARS AGO there was a poll to determine in what aspects
of religion laymen were interested. Out of fifty items the largest
vote went to the topic, "How to Make Prayer Effective," while
the smallest vote went to the item, "How Christians Can Im-
prove Society." Some would use this result to prove that our
religion is an escape mechanism; others, that it would substanti-
ate the observation that religion begins with prayer and ends
in politics. If such is the case we obviously have a long way to
go!

The fact is, however, that there is no religious subject on
which there is more felt need than making prayer effective. The
need is real, and I am convinced that the first and the fiftieth
items, and all the ones in between, belong together. To pray
aright is to live aright. To make prayer effective is to make it
central to a genuine life. Man is right only in relation to his
Maker. To make that relation right man needs prayer.

On my last sabbatical leave I spent a year traveling around
the world. One observation stands out: everywhere was prayer.
The flourishing new religions in Japan use prayer more than do
the old. In Borneo I first heard the muezzin wail his call from the

53

minaret, calling the faithful Muslims to prayer. It came to me
with a weird piercing power. In India our windows overlooked
the major branch of the Ganges, the Hooghly River, as it runs out
to sea, carrying, it seemed to me, a constant cargo of prayer from
the myriad worshipers bathing in its stream and along its banks.
Then on through the Near East we were embedded in the en-
vironment of prayer. In Europe and America too, in the many
places where we stayed, everywhere prayer.

And yet in spite of all this praying, our lives and our world
are riven and torn. No wonder the first question on the laymen's
poll was how to make prayer effective!

Obviously, prayer is not enough. There is enough prayer of
the kind that already exists. How, then, can prayer become
effective?

I

From our text we can learn, first of all, that Samuel prayed
for the people. Only the prayer of concern is effective. Right
prayer is genuine care. True prayer is love's trusting God, for the
people.

The world is full of wrong prayer. Wrong prayer hurts us and
hurts the world. God is still saying to us, "Take away the multi-
tude of your prayers. They are a stench in my nostrils. I will not
hear them, for your hands are full of blood." Prayer all too often
is an aggression on both God and man. It often is a matter of
promoting or protecting the self or the ingroup to which we
belong. Such prayer may be exceedingly subtle. It may make
use of phrases that conceal even from ourselves the basic magic
by which we try to get our own way, offensively or defensively.
Perhaps most praying is of this nature. Therefore it blinds our
eyes, weakens our wills, and takes the place of our work. By
such prayer we make our lives and the world worse instead of
better.

But Samuel centered his prayer in the people's needs. He
loved his people and lived for them. Therefore he prayed for
them. Samuel opened his own life to God's presence, guidance,
and power. God used Samuel to help his people. But more,

through Samuel's concern for the people God could act on behalf
of his people. The rains could come even out of season as the
sign and token of God's presence and power not only to but
through a man of concerned prayer.

Prayer becomes effective when we live concerned lives for the
people. Only lives centered in the needs of others can become
lives of effective prayer. Such lives God uses for the people's
good; and because such lives offer their freedom on behalf of
the people, God reaches down within the common life of man's
inner, corporate freedom to work on behalf of the people. The
history of the lives of the saints, those who lived concerned lives
for the people, shows that God answers prayer not for the good
of the pray-ers, in any external sense, but for the most genuine
good of the people. Most prayer is ineffective, not because of any
lack of skill or technique, but simply and solely because it is
not genuinely centered in the people. Only concerned prayer
is effective.

II

Samuel prayed for the people. His prayers did not center in
his own needs or drives. But he never made the mistake, it
seems, of thinking that his concern could save his people. *His
trust was in God.* He prayed for and expected God's help.
He merely let himself be used by God for the people, be it by
prayer or be it by action.

Therefore Samuel did not only say, "Far be it from me that
I should sin against the Lord by ceasing to pray for you." He
trusted God. Sin it was and nothing less for Samuel to stop praying for his people. Concern is not enough to make prayer effective.
Concern must center in trust. In one sense our only faith comes
from God's love. It comes from concern, God's concern for the
world. Without such love, faith even great enough to remove
mountains is of no worth. Trust in God avails nothing if it is
selfish. Only faith moved by love counts. Such faith is precisely
trust in God in connection with one's concern for the people.

Samuel loved the people and trusted God to help them. He
prayed for them and even when his own leadership was re-

jected he kept on praying. Our prayer is often ineffective because it arises from involvement with our own circles of concern,
not with God's great love for the world. True Christian prayer
is as inclusive as the boundless love of God. It reaches up in
trust to God from whom comes not only every good and perfect
gift but first of all his own gift of himself, summarized and
symbolized in Jesus Christ. His healing love, his helping love,
his love unto the death of the cross, his endless love conquering
even death itself—in such love true prayer centers in simple,
receiving trust.

If you really want to find out how to make prayer effective,
commit your total life to that Christ. Let that God become the
concerned center of your life. Keep trusting him, as your prayer
goes up and out for the people, for God's people, for all the
creatures and children of his love. Humbly accept yourself, your
own needs, and the needs of those especially dear to you, and
accept your own responsibilities within that unconditional
concern of God for the whole world. Then trust God and keep
trusting. Trust God and keep praying. Trust God and keep witnessing and working, under him for the people.

Then "make but trial of his love; experience will decide."
Sow much, sow freely, sow often, and keep sowing and waiting,
keep sowing and trusting. Then seek humbly to understand the
faithfulness of God in answering prayer. Such is the biblical formula for making prayer effective: "Far be it from me that I
should sin against the Lord by ceasing to pray for you."

III

Samuel not only prayed for the people, trusting God, but he
kept on praying. Keeping on praying is the secret of prayer.
Especially Samuel kept on praying for the people even though
they kept on sinning. A reasonable conclusion to reach might be
that prayer does not work. If a farmer keeps on seeding and
keeps on seeding and there seems to be no harvest worth his
while, he should know enough to stop sowing at least that kind
of seed in that field. But prayer is not a work of reason, depending on visible results. Prayer is a cry of the heart, a cry of con-

cern for the people. Not to care is to sin against love. Not to pray is to sin against the Lord by failing to trust him.

One almost dares say that the deeper and fuller the prayer the greater the failure. The more the prayer enters into God's total concern and the more man lives that concern, the harder it is to be answered and the more likely man is to fail. Small prayers may find small answers or small failures. As the prayers rise to the greatness and goodness of God, beyond imagination, they fall ever short of their concern. Even humanly great answers are but dismal failures in comparison to the full human needs and the immeasurable resources of God beyond those needs. But the fact of the matter is that the people usually keep sinning, as Samuel discovered, and even persistence in prayer seems to be of no avail.

But precisely then it is that prayer counts. The person of true prayer, prayer that rises from genuine concern and from authentic trust in God, cannot but keep on. He dare not sin against God by ceasing to pray for the people. Thus both the pray-er and the prayer become deepened and strengthened in the trust that counts. Moses prayed for his people, and in the end failed to do more than merely see the promised land himself— but the people entered it. Samuel prayed for the people, who kept sinning, who rejected his leadership and went their own way, but he became the builder in the background of a great nation and the anointer of King David. Jesus prayed for his people and ended on a cross, with the people standing by watching and his own disciples forsaking him. But the power of the man and his prayers found the center of history in God and founded the human community of universal Love through trust in God which is the very meaning of life and the only way to human fulfillment. The more we, too, raise our sights unto the heavenly lights of God's universal Love for all people and peoples, praying continually in concerned trust, the more, too, we may seem to fail, but like them, the more we shall be given grace to touch human lives with helping power and human history with healing light.

God never forces human freedom. Prayer cannot be a matter of cause and consequence. If such were the case neither human freedom nor sin would be real. But they are, gloriously and disastrously real. All we can do in prayer, therefore, is first of all offer ourselves to become changed, and then offer our freedom—insofar as we are one with others in the total organism of humanity—as a means through which God can reach others, throw new light on their path, show them new choices, and provide them the power to implement those choices. But choose for them we cannot. Only lives lived long with God and tried over the long stretches of human time can authentically extend to others in freedom God's invitation to pilgrimage. The richer the promises the harder to believe them and the more grievously prayer is likely to fail, but conversely, the deeper and more real is the truth of God offered in concern and trust, and the more telling and lasting in the long run will be such prayers. For prayer to become effective we must therefore keep on praying even though, as we are changed and our vision is changed, we become the more removed from our people whom we love.

IV

Outgoing prayers do help. God answers them in his way and in his time. Sometimes I myself have felt like cursing the day when I first became convicted of the power of prayer and convinced that I dared not escape its burden of concern. The more I prayed, the worse I seemed to myself. The more deeply I prayed for the world, the more I kept discovering that I never really cared very deeply for the world. What I found was my own unworthiness as a person, my sinfulness and impotence in the face of God and the world's needs. I am still learning that lesson and I do not like it.

Further I discovered that if I kept praying within the grace of God, with even the little concern and trust that I could receive, the more I became separated from many of my professional colleagues and friends. The theology of God's power for the world and of man's hope in him did not jibe with the reigning theology of despair. The self-termed realists called such faith in God "optimism" with no relevance for a day of pessimism. But actually faith in God is neither optimism nor pessimism, but the truest of all realism. Prayer may fail dismally in man's sight; that is true realism. But no true prayer rises to God in concern for the people and trust in him that God does not answer in some way. Therefore I have been willing to choose a lonely road. Often occasions from which I had hoped some word of approval or professional recognition went by with hard work and little human appreciation, but with later discoveries that individuals had been touched by God's grace to go on doing his work in his way and in their own way. No one should undertake the prayer of concern for the people through trust in God who dares not walk a lonely way and who will not quietly accept, if need be, the humble way of human failure.

The deeper the failure, the stronger God's help. The more we expect from God and keep setting our hearts and our trust on it, the more God will use our prayers. Hardest to conquer is our human desire to be in on the result, to know that it came through us, and to build on such evidence of the power of prayer. Prayer becomes effective when we venture far out on the promises of God, keep venturing in concerned trust, and then end our lives by trusting God and caring genuinely for the people. If you really want to become effective in prayer, this prescription is from the heart of God and will continually prove true in your inner experience, as you seek not your own, but the welfare of the people within your trust of God.

V

Samuel prayed for the people. He kept on praying in concerned trust. He could not sin against the Lord by ceasing to pray for them even when they kept on sinning. But Samuel did not stop with prayer. Prayer is never enough. Prayer is not enough, even concerned prayer within trust in God. Samuel went on to instruction in righteousness. "I will instruct you," he told his people, "in the good and the right way." True prayer requires study and life.

I have to confess that I find it hard to like· a lot of people who pray. I don't say they are hypocrites, substituting prayer for

thought and deed, but they tend to be outwardly pious and offensively religious. Jesus told his disciples to go into their room
and pray in secret; then to fix themselves up so that no one
could tell from their appearance that they had been religious
(Matt. 6:5–6, 16–18). Usually pious people's piety sticks out
all over them and tends to create a barrier. Often these good
folk talk and act as though they had all the truth directly from
God and as though they set the standard for morality.

Prayer should be a way of living authentically with God and
men so as to be genuine with them and with ourselves in all
our shortcomings. When we are real we know how much we
need to study. Then our anti-intellectualism or spurious intellectualism is revealed to us and we commit ourselves to the
pursuit of intellectual excellence. Prayer can be taken as a
shortcut to knowledge. It is the way we find out how to go God's
way. But God gave us a mind for a purpose. No good doctor
prays himself into a successful medical practice; he had
better go to medical school. No competent engineer learns how
to build skyscrapers by merely praying; he had better study
strains and stresses and the whole craft of building. Some ministers think they can substitute prayer for preparation.

Samuel went beyond prayer to instruct his people. Our
churches would have more power if they dared to undertake the
hard discipline of intellectual endeavor. A large part of Christian
endeavor is decidedly mental endeavor. In many a pulpit now
we have sophisticated intellectuals who know little or nothing
about prayer and who therefore serve up some warmed-over
secularism in place of Christian doctrine. Such churches often
have discussion groups and even so-called study groups, but
little power to feed the hungry soul or change the sinful world.
Or on the other hand we have this or that retreat group based
on prayer, sometimes Christian, often half Hindu or something
else mystical, but with little critical reason dedicated to the
direction of life and civilization. What we need is to join together the two sides of prayer and study. Then we shall have
Saint Pauls and Saint Augustines, Luthers, Calvins and Wesleys
to guide us, and shall celebrate the wedding throughout the

length and breadth of the church of what our forefathers called piety and wisdom.

Samuel's instruction was in the good and the right way. It was no arid intellectualism. Neither prayer nor study can take the place of living. Both prayer and study are rather for the sake of life. Christ came to give life and more life. Prayer and study are both for life and for more life. They are for better life. We need to study and to walk in the good and the right. For that matter, only the prayer of the righteous man has power. Only the prayer that leads to righteousness has power. Without righteousness both the man who prays and his prayer are sham. If you want your prayer to become effective, find concern and trust, pray for the people to God, but get up from your prayer to study and to teach, and above all to live your prayer.

A professor in a theological seminary asked a fellow professor whether he prayed for the students. "Oh, yes," was his reply. "I *do* something for them instead," said the first professor. But it is not a matter of prayer *or* deed. There must be both.

We began with the comment that true religion begins in prayer and ends in politics. True religion finds, through concern for the people and within trust in God, the way to study and to teach the kind of righteousness of life and civilization that lifts both to a new level. Prayer is the leaven of the total life of man. One of Britain's leading social reformers who had read and liked my book, *Christianity and Society,* almost literally hit the roof when he read my *Strengthening the Spiritual Life.* On the other hand, most people who read the latter appreciatively would never bother to read the former.

How can we get people to go on from the first item in the poll, "How to Make Prayer Effective," to the last item chosen, "How Christianity Can Change Society"? For prayer to become fully effective we must somehow travel in study and deed the whole way from the heart of God to the needs of men. We must live our faith in worship, study, giving, social concern, and personal walking in the way of responsible obedience. Such prayer with inquiry and work makes us free toward God and effective in both personal living and social outreach. Such is the reality and richness of the grace of God.

There can be no question of the healing and helping power of right prayer. My recommendation for the fuller and better exercise of it is utterly simple:

Be concerned.

Trust God.

Keep on praying.

Follow up your prayer with study and work.

I know prayer is real and that it works. We can become effective in prayer if we let God use our freedom. So can our families and our churches. Then "far be it from me that I should sin against the Lord by ceasing to pray for you."

7.

Getting a New Heart

Then the spirit of the Lord will come mightily upon you, and you shall prophesy with them and be turned into another man. . . . God gave him another heart. 1 Samuel 10:6, 9.

LONG BEFORE this age of heart transplants, humanity has been concerned with getting a new heart. We speak of a change of heart, "heart" meaning affections, desires, innermost intention. That God can give people a new direction of heart we know. Saul was transformed from an ardent, zealous Pharisee to an ardent, zealous Christian. But it was still the same Saul even though they called him Paul. He had a new direction, a new cause, but his old ardent, zealous self was beating in the same way. His heart was beating the same.

In this sense, the heart is the disposition we have, the affections with which we meet life. It is almost as though a man fell in love with a new girl. There is no change in the man, but he has a new direction for his affection. In this sense it is obvious that we can get a new heart.

Or, secondly, we can learn to accept and live with the old heart. Some people seem to have been freed from the kind of entanglement or frustration that once beset them. I remember reading with horror and fascination an anonymously written book, *A Spectacle of a Man*, where the counseling experience of a patient is described over two years. A young, frustrated bach-

elor who was very shy and blushed even to look at a girl, within
a couple of years' counseling learned to sleep indiscriminately
with any woman, without any conscience at all. He was considered cured. In other words, he had the same heart but somehow he had learned to adjust himself differently. Some people
react that way as far as their own self-acceptance is concerned.
Many people have learned in marriage that they can never
change their spouse and vice versa. They have learned that no
matter how both try to be different, somehow or other they
remain themselves and have to learn to put up with each other.

Once I visited a Trappist monastery in Iowa. This order requires a vow of silence. We asked the one brother who was
permitted to speak to visitors what was the hardest experience
of being a Trappist monk. Was it the silence? He said, "It is
being saddled with one person from two-thirty in the morning
until late at night; going through everything together and knowing you won't be able to be rid of him—especially if you love
to sing and he sings off key. But somehow we have to learn to
put up with it."

Sometimes, when we learn this kind of self-acceptance, the
heart that we get is of such a nature that we do not criticize
others the way we used to, because we know it is useless to
expect them to change. We learn to accept both ourselves and
the situation. This, however, is not what our text is about.

I

God gave Saul a new heart in the sense that he turned him
into another man. Saul not only performed certain rules of obedience, but he also met the prophets and prophesied with them
so that it became a proverb: Is Saul also among the prophets?
Somehow he became a new man in the sense of his responsibility, in the sense of his attitude, in the sense that he lived. I
have become convinced that this can happen, but I am not
going to say that it can happen easily. I think we know ourselves,
and we can all look into our own hearts to know to what extent
we genuinely have become different selves. I know that if this

is going to happen to me, *God,* not I, has to do it. At least I know that I have tried over the years to change certain things in myself. I have wanted to be different. I have prayed and I have offered up my subconscious. I have offered up everything, and still somehow or other these dispositional patterns seem to be there. They seem to be so hard to overcome. There seems to be no easy way to pray and say, "Here I am. Make me a new man." As soon as we come into that particular troublesome situation again, we find, much to our disappointment, that we are very much the same.

Then what are we going to do about it? I believe that all of us, if we are genuinely convinced that we should be God's people, want to become completely concerned with his concerns. The Holy Spirit can work in us and through us beyond anything that we can explain or understand. I have learned over the years what Paul means when he says that his sufficiency was not of himself, but his sufficiency was of God. I have learned that God's strength can be revealed even through our weakness, or perhaps particularly through our weakness.

All my life I have prayed that everything I do be put into God's hands, that I have no concern about anything except God's will. It is not *my* work, I keep saying; it is *God's* work. The only thing that matters is God's work, helping people, helping humanity to become different. For thirty years I have written books, and each time I have said, "This is your book, Father, and I put it into your hands." But just the same I still find it terribly hard not to be more interested in my own book reviews than in somebody else's—my heart beats faster!

Somehow or other we are involved in this human frailty and we can't escape it. I suppose it is a good thing, from one point of view, that we cannot escape it. But I have become convinced, I have learned from experience, that we can actually put our work in God's hands and say, "I have done my best. I know it is *your* work. I am thankful for it. Here it is." When others appropriate my lifework, or say what I have said persistently without giving a hint of credit, then I know how old or how new my heart is! Then being glad for God's cause *counts.*

II

God can give us a new heart and he can give us relief from self-interest. He can give us peace. He can give us his presence. It doesn't come easily. The "old man" is still working, but God can do it.

God does not give us a new heart, however, by sheer miracle. There is no cheap grace. There is no such thing as "flip-the-pancake" repentance. There is no such thing as a "second blessing" that comes only once. Now, I'm not saying that there can be no such thing as a second blessing; I am not now speaking theologically in this sense. I am saying that it does not come easily. I am saying that every blessing that God gives comes out of great suffering, out of great trial, out of great temptation, out of long, long tempering until God, knowing what needs to be done, gives us such relief as he sees best. The Holy Spirit can give us a new heart.

As I was reading Charles S. Sherrington's great Gifford Lectures, *Man on His Nature,* something he said captured me:

"Experiments indicate that the abrupt change in transmitted 'characters' spoken of in genetics as 'mutation' can be brought about by 'radiation' applied to a gene. A modification of the gene-molecule induced by absorption of an energy-quantum would seem then to reproduce itself under the self-fermentation of the molecule." *

As I read this I was thinking of all the radioactivity set loose by bomb testing and of the tremendous fear that our children and children's children are going to be handicapped, and of the great longing of our hearts to do away with such testing. But I was thinking of something else, too. If this is the way mutations come about, can it not be that if we are ready and open to God, he can construct new mutations we haven't dreamed about? Insofar as we and our children's children respond to this stimulus, why should we look at this unknown thing, radiation, merely in terms of fear and not also in terms of faith?

If we are open, if we are ready, it doesn't matter whether we

* 2nd ed. (Cambridge: Cambridge University Press, 1953), pp. 103–104.

are eighty-five or fifteen. God can make young men dream dreams and old men see visions, or old men dream dreams and young men see visions. God can take all of us, each of us, and do the thing which is most necessary today, that is, get us into right alignment with him. This new quality content, this new relationship can change the world. When Jesus came into the world, revealing the Father, the world was changed. When Saint Francis lived his life, the whole Middle Ages changed. When a few individuals find the right relationship with God, this thing happens. If you want a scientific explanation, read Teilhard de Chardin's fascinating book *The Phenomenon of Man.* *

III

Here is our situation: God is waiting to give us a new age. God is waiting to give us a new heart. He can give us a new age only insofar as we are ready to receive new hearts. New hearts come only in right relationship to him, when the quality of his life, his power, his indwelling fills us and takes hold of us and we become new men. He makes even our failures bless the world, and we do get a new heart. When God changes our heart, he discards the old one. He does away with it. He doesn't take it for himself. He gives us of his heart, of his spirit. We can become new persons, new communities, new civilizations insofar as we let ourselves be changed by the indwelling power of God's grace.

A University of Chicago sociologist once said that three people, if they are fully committed and open, can change any church. Nearly twenty years ago, when I first moved to what became to me a beloved Southland, I prayed God to take away the separating curtain in the dining car. I saw a most beautiful, radiant black face above a clerical collar and I wanted to join him and I didn't dare to. When I mentioned this to my friends, they said, "Be realistic, it cannot happen." But soon it did.

Later, when preaching at the Chicago Sunday Evening Club

* New York: Harper & Row, 1951.

I said, in effect, "Trust God to take care of Protestant-Catholic relations. Something can happen; God can do something with the stodgy old Catholic church." Friends reproached me, "Nels, be realistic. You know the Catholic church will never change." And then God raised up Pope John. But the movement is more than Pope John. I know from having participated in it myself. There is something deeply fundamental going on in the Catholic church in terms of reliance on the Holy Spirit, such as I have never seen before. The church has a new heart. Even recent setbacks under a more defensive pope cannot retard the stream of the Spirit that has been flooding the church.

So we can go on from one area to another. Take the question of peace. People said, "It's impossible to get the two great blocs together and really undertake the question of banning the bomb." I am not promising that this is going to happen, because it all depends upon how we use our freedom. But we were perhaps never nearer than we are right now to the possibility of avoiding world catastrophe, because God is moving upon the face of the earth. Is our nation ready to receive a new heart?

You yourself can be of world significance insofar as you offer yourself in full faith and full dedication to the quality of God's indwelling, and in prayer, witness, and work relate yourself to the coming of his kingdom. If we put our hand into the hand of God and trust him to change us in his way, he will give us a new heart; he will make us new men; he will bring us a new age.

When I was a child in Sweden, my beloved preacher father used to sing joyously, "*Vi maste byta hjärta, min frälsare och jag.*" "We must exchange hearts, my Savior and I." In my childish mind I didn't want Jesus to get my heart! God's heart for the world is so real and rich it can provide us with a "new heart," a new spirit! Only when God's heart of universal Love gives mankind a new heart for universal man shall we avoid catastrophe and usher in God's new age of cooperative and creative community.

8.

A Defense for God?

Will you speak falsely for God, and speak deceitfully for him? Will you show partiality toward him, will you plead the case for God? Job 13:7–8.

WILL A MAN speak falsely for God? Lie in God's behalf? Are you hired partisans resolved to acquit him? Does God need Perry Mason? Does God need a good trial lawyer? Can God be defended by man?

We may ask, can faith ever in any deep sense be proved? Faith by nature faces the dilemma of choosing between reliable evidence and radical risk. Without risk there is no trust. He who "knows all the answers" has no faith. What he has is obviously not faith but knowledge. But on the other hand, without some evidence faith hardly finds justification.

I

Is there any way that faith can find some way of living that combines both radical risk and reliable evidence, or are they by nature completely and constantly contrary? In defining faith Tertullian said, "*Credo quia incredibile est.*" "I believe because it is unbelievable." Scholars usually translate this "absurd"— incredible because it cannot be justified. And Luther said, "Reason is a whore."

Søren Kierkegaard illustrated the superiority of faith over reason in his famous story of the rich man who was riding across the moors of Denmark one beautiful starlit night, having in his carriage a very bright lamp by which he could see ever so clearly only his own feet. A peasant, however, not having a carriage or a lantern, trudged contentedly in the dim light of the night sky and had opened to him more and more the incredible vastness of the universe and the starry spaces.

But faith for faith's sake is not enough. *Fides qua* always needs *fides quae;* that is to say, the things *by* which we believe always need to know something *of* the things we do believe. Some of you may recall the newspaper account of a. devout believer in a little church in the hills of Tennessee who with deep commitment and trust, repeating verses from the Gospel of Mark, drank the cup of poison that his pastor passed him, and immediately died. At the funeral, his widow said, "He died from too much faith."

You see, we must ask, "What is the nature of faith?" "In what do we believe?" as well as "By what intensity do we believe?" Tor Andrae, that great scholar of the history of religion from Uppsala University in Sweden, tells how a group of anthropologists went to Africa and found a tribe that believed that their gods were far on the other side of a, for them, impassable mountain. The scientists said, "Well, we now have means by which we can take you there. Won't you come along and see if the gods are there?" They replied, "Oh no; if we do we might find that they aren't, and then we would have no gods to worship."

Professor Andrae said that this is the great illustration of *trotz alles,* or *quand même,* that is, in spite of everything or nevertheless—for such is the highest nature of faith. I wonder! This certainly is radical risk; but can faith live also without reliable evidence? I believe that faith does need reliable evidence.

If I need to borrow money, I'd much rather trust a good bank than some stranger, however generous he sounded. It might be more risky to trust him than the bank. When one of our children has difficulty in school with the "new math," we trust a teacher of mathematics to help rather than risk helping ourselves with our antiquated methods. You see, such trusting has more reliable evidence.

But if such trust becomes completely knowledge, there is no longer any faith left, none at all. You aren't really believing. The more you *know,* in one sense, the less you *believe.* You know!

Particularly true is this dilemma of faith in the case of religion. We all have to have faith. Life itself is a venture of faith. The ultimate is the highest presupposition of our lives; and the highest presupposition simply cannot be proved, because if you proved it, it would no longer be the highest presupposition! If God could be proved, he obviously would have to be proved in terms of something more real than God, in which case he would not be God.

No one can possibly relate himself to the ultimate nature of things, to the highest configuration or presupposition of his life, apart from a daring faith judgment. Every person has to have faith and every person in this sense is religious. The only question is, what is the nature of his faith? How does he combine radical risk with reliable evidence?

If we don't have reliable evidence, faith seems merely capricious, based on mere chance, circumstance, prejudice, or inheritance. Now the best faith in ultimate matters would be one in which the more radical risk there is, the more reliable evidence would be produced, and conversely, the more one followed reliable evidence, the more he would come to radical risk.

Let us put it another way. The highest possible faith is one which most fully combines meaning and mystery. Apart from meaning, there cannot even be a mystery. That is obvious. But if meaning is pushed to its very limits, we shall find that the further we push it, the deeper is the mystery.

On the other hand, however, if we accept the fact that we as finite beings have to live by mystery, the more we say to ourselves that we want something that is real and genuine, something with which we are not merely fooling ourselves, the more we have somehow or other to find meaning and reliable evidence.

II

The problem is how are we going to go about this? How is
it possible to combine radical risk with reliable evidence? I am
going to mention two ways that I cannot accept, honoring the
people who hold them, but not being able myself to share in
these faiths; and then I shall try to suggest a way in terms of
which this dilemma is at least genuinely faced. As a free and
mature human being, think it through for yourself and judge
whether this way approaches a solution.

Traditionalistic Christianity, in the first place, becomes more
and more a matter of radical risk without reliable evidence.
Traditionalistic Christianity is becoming increasingly isolated
from man's best knowledge. By "traditionalistic" I mean an un-
sophisticated, indiscriminate acceptance of the traditional or
biblical faith, so-called orthodoxy.

To begin with, let me give an illustration. Many years ago I
stood next to a fine, intelligent minister of traditionalist faith, a
person with whom I could feel real identification and rapport,
at St. Croix Falls, one of nature's wonder spots between Min-
nesota and Wisconsin. As we looked together down into those
vast caverns that the river has made over the millions of years,
this man, a university graduate, sighed, "Nels, when I look
down into those deep caves, I could very easily be tempted to
give up my biblical faith and become a modernist, remember-
ing my course in geology at the university; but then I say to
myself, the devil put these caverns here in order to tempt my
faith." His faith required him to believe in creation six thousand
years ago. In his case modern knowledge increased radical
risk, as far as creation was concerned, but by repudiating it he
forfeited the support of reliable evidence.

Secondly, as far as the present social and political situation is
concerned, the mood of traditionalistic Christianity, generally
speaking, is one of status quo "staticism." By this I mean that
traditionalism accepts too much the nature of the world as it
now is and defends the status quo; and such "staticism" is bound
to lead necessarily to the eventual destruction of the world

that threatens us and that we are trying to avert. What we need now is a creative faith that by facing every problem realistically in every realm of life, will lead us to a new day. Traditionalistic Christianity is too much identified with the past even in the present.

Thirdly, its view of the future is unrealistic and immoral. The conception that Jesus is going to come to save a few people and put the rest to eternal torture is obviously such a view of eternal segregation as to be reprehensible to any morally alive and morally worthy person. It is an unworthy view of God and an unworthy view of his ways with the world. In spite of all my identification with and understanding of those who hold this faith, and my familiarity with their background and commitments, it seems to me that this faith increases radical risk at the expense of explanatory adequacy and at the expense of moral worthiness.

Therefore those of us who seek the kind of religion that is both morally worthy and intellectually mature and responsible, if possible, cannot take radical risks of this nature apart from reliable evidence. The defenders of traditionalism have to "lie for God." They are partisans resolved to acquit him, but their arguments are tortured. They have taken radical risk without reliable evidence. In the long last many of them come down to this statement: Can't God be God and do anything he wants? I submit to you that this is a proposition unworthy of God. God is reliable. God is worthy.

III

If I cannot accept traditionalistic Christianity, no more, on the opposite side, can I accept secular humanism, by which I mean accepting our so-called best knowledge as faith. We all have to adjust ourselves to ultimate matters, and we have to do so in some way. Some people simply accept knowledge and use that as their faith, but obviously this is not knowledge in the ultimate sense. It is only faith. When knowledge is turned into the ultimate presupposition it becomes faith.

A few years ago the Anglican bishop John A. T. Robinson created a sensation by his book *Honest to God.** To be "honest to God" he explains why he gave up as superstitious the tradition of his Christian faith. He says that traditionalistic Christianity is mostly a matter of spatialization. Perhaps he doesn't quite do justice to most thinking people, because I doubt that many think of God as sitting somewhere or floating somewhere in space. And for that matter, as far as I am concerned, to talk about direction is one thing but to talk about dimension is scarcely another. Both are spatial terms. For a person to say he is no longer going to talk about direction, he is going to talk about dimension, does not mean that he has escaped spatialization. I don't see how any human being can talk except in space-time terms. We know nothing else!

Bishop Robinson was saying something, however, that is quite genuine in the sense that he can no longer believe in *a* God—he can no longer be a theist. To some extent he is using the word "theism" as "deism" ought to be used. He is using the word incorrectly. But to say *a* God would make God a finite object among other objects while God by definition is infinite. Therefore he cannot be *a* God, he cannot be *a* person, he cannot be *a* spirit, he cannot be the God who answers prayer. If God in any way answers prayer, he is a God of Christian providence; as such he is intruding in the universe and manipulating things. For this reason Bishop Robinson has given up the traditional point of view.

He uses as authorities Rudolf Bultmann, who says that even a schoolboy knows that there is no God who answers prayer, and Paul Tillich, who says that we must outgrow all this kind of superstition by considering God "the ground of being"; not a personal God who answers prayer and who directs the universe, but rather the one who is the logical presupposition for being and who has and is the power for harmony of being. God is then the impersonal, transpersonal God rather than the God of traditional Christianity.

* Philadelphia: Westminster Press, 1963.

Bonhoeffer, too, although he has been much misused, says that now we don't need the hypothesis of God any more, that the world has come of age and we no longer need God. These thinkers are saying that if we are going to be honest about modern knowledge, we can no longer believe in the God who is a personal spirit and the God who answers prayer. In other words, this God is "out" for honest modern man; Christianity in this sense has failed him. They want a faith that has reliable evidence without the ultimate radical risk. They want a faith in line with our best knowledge and limited, apart from such knowledge, to a kind of reverent agnosticism.

But as far as I am concerned, they have fallen prey to what I call "scientism," not to be confused with science. The faith that assumes evolution *as explanation* as well as description is obviously a mystique rather than a reasoned, empirical faith. The most we can say is that the history of creation reveals, discloses, that which we did not know previously was or could be. As we, therefore, come along to those higher reaches of meaning, we begin to see in terms of those meanings; and it is only in terms of those meanings that we begin to have any understanding, any glimpse, any explanation, of the meaning of anything. Since we must make some kind of explanation, because even to live is to assume an ultimate faith, it seems clear that a creative being or creative spirit at the heart of things better explains what we do know than any merely doctrinistic naturalism, than any mere thinking that does away with meaning, that does away with love, that does away with life as the best clue to the world we do know.

Notice that none of these people does anything with the question of *how* all this came to be. They have no protology. Read them carefully and see. None of them, either, does anything basically with eschatology, that is, with what is going to happen in the long future. They are merely concerned about the present moment and the existentialist understanding of it in the light of such explanations as may be available. Therefore, for those who want a deeper and fuller plowing into the nature of reality, this faith, I believe, will not do. It is a faith, but a faith that is not as full and as adequate as we need. Secular humanism is a mood of faith rather than an honest confrontation of our best knowledge in terms of ultimate explanation.

IV

What then? If I cannot accept traditionalistic Christianity in this limited sense, and if I cannot possibly accept a kind of mystique such as secular humanism, then what? The highest, best belief in God as ultimate integrity and ultimate concern is to me the fullest explanation of the meaning of existence.

I was brought up a fundamentalist. I knelt by my bedside my junior year in college after having tried my utmost to see if there was any way I could honestly hold on to the faith in which I was reared. Finally I said, "Oh, if there is anything anywhere, help me to be honest with myself, and help me not to fool myself, but to be real, to be genuine."

I have come to the conclusion, after digging and thinking and comparing, that no alternative of faith gives more explanatory adequacy, as well as more direction and more motivation, to the life which all of us have to live than the heart of the Christian faith, ultimate integrity and ultimate concern. Our history is a drop in eternity. Unless we see somehow that out of eternity has come this creative process where the history of creation is the history of revelation, seen most fully in the spirit of Jesus in his concern for men and resulting in the open, inclusive, and concerned community—unless we see *that*, we have not seen, I believe, the great unfolding of a divine purpose; nor do we have that radical motivation in *agape*, God's love, by which we can conserve what is good in society and at the same time insist upon that kind of constructive revolution apart from which we shall not remain on earth as human beings.

We have to have a revolution. The only question is whether the revolution is going to be one that is apart from faith, apart from responsibility, apart from meaning—a socially motivated revolution that will not solve our problems in the long run—or the kind of revolution that is in line with responsible concern, with integrity, and with trust and faith in ultimate reality.

I frankly admit, therefore, that I have no understanding of the meaning of existence, the meaning of life, apart from God's longer work beyond this life. The more I come to understand the meaning of this life, the more I become completely frustrated if all those meanings are nipped off by death. As Professor Ford of Harvard asked one day in a small discussion group, "Can you give us a theology of history? Because in my philosophies of history all fundamental meanings are nipped off by death."

I have come to believe that the resurrection—or the deepest meaning of God's long future where, although we cannot even envisage what he has in store for us, we can lead our lives with confidence in his fulfillment of our lives, the fulfillment of the process that he adopted—is alone adequate fully to account for the long process we do know. I believe that only in resurrection faith can we be in line with the fullest meaning of things and find the motivation that shall make life worthwhile. The meanings we do have point to the longer and larger horizon of fulfillment beyond death and beyond our cosmic process.

The more meaning I see in life, the more the mystery grows. These meanings have their present reality and urgency, but the more real and urgent they are in this life, the more they bespeak their own eventual fulfillment. I stand dumbfounded thinking of the long future. And the more I am willing to lose myself in the mystery of that life, that spirit that I have seen, and in the understanding of that concern which is ultimate, unconditional and all-conclusive, the more I see that mystery, the more meaning I get, the more I understand *why* suffering, *why* the Cross, *why* evil. Only in this kind of concern can we be set free by the fullest implications of the highest truth we know.

The creative and the critical reasons somehow must go together. The creative reason which is always faith, and the critical reason which deals with science, with the empirical, must somehow go together. Only then are we going to approach a solution.

Should we try to "lie for God," in the sense that in the depths of our hearts, if we cannot accept traditionalistic Christianity, we will try to have some kind of weakened version of it and try to justify it in terms of arguments which are even more specious, spurious, and ultimately inadequate? Should we not instead find that high faith in God which genuinely tries to combine radical risk with reliable evidence, which faces the meaning of what we do know and pursues it into ever deeper mystery?

Directing our whole life in that eternal mystery which engenders our individual and cosmic loneliness, shall we not also find that rich reality of meaning within which we can live with our families and our fellow-men? May God bless us to find that reality for which we were born, to which we are called, and within which alone we and those we love will find fulfillment.

9.

When God Acts

It is time for the Lord to act. Psalm 119:126.

WE STAND TODAY confronting the most critical hour in human history. In the face of human history today, some are frustrated. They simply feel that nothing can be done about it. Some of the most serious thinkers I know believe that, in spite of every positive effort that is being made and can be made, human nature is such that sooner or later, we shall stumble and fall. This is the destruction; this is the denouement; this is the final moment of human history. I cannot persuade them that a realistic person can believe, human nature being what it is, that we do have a chance to survive. They stand there hopeless, helpless, frustrated.

Others simply stand confused. They don't know. Part of them hopes, part of them fears. Part of them asks, "Can I do anything?" Another part answers, "Nothing can be done." Still a third part declares, "I can do something, but I don't know what. How can I live effectively in a world like this?"

I

There are still a few, however, who believe that God is not

dead, who stand expectant of God's new age. I am talking about
the real God. I don't mean some kind of general influence. I
don't mean some kind of emotional quality coming out of human
togetherness. This kind of reduction of faith, escaping behind
facile and unreal arguments, stands judged before the Lord
Almighty.

God is the God of creation. God is the God of human history.
God is the God of human destiny. Because God lives, there is
genuine hope for human history. God can act and God is going
to act.

God has only been waiting for sufficient response of obedience
and trust on the part of his people. We can be the means of letting the will of God in its positive, constructive sense be done,
because *history is flexible to faith*. What do I mean? "According
to your faith be it done unto you" is sheer practical realism, not
only in an individualistic sense, but in a total corporate sense. As
we together do or fail to do the will of God, so will human history be.

"It is time for the Lord to act." There are a lot of people cry-
ing aloud and rending themselves like Baal's prophets, thinking
God may be asleep and that if they holler some more he will
come alive and begin to do something. What we need today are
not these false prophets. We need the Elijahs, who can very simply pour water upon the sacrifice and say, "Now, God, you aren't
asleep; you aren't impotent; and therefore we will trust your
way, not ours."

Why is it time for the Lord to act? It is time for the Lord to
act because man has brought God's work to naught. Man has
not kept God's law, man has broken God's law. We have not
taken advantage of God's promises, of his goodness.

How many of us, how many all over the world, are dilettantes
when it comes to religion? At one hour in church on Sunday we
are "religious." Next morning, even next hour we are something
else. And yet we hope that somehow or other things will come
out right. We give a little bit now and a little bit then. But if
there is anything in the world that is true, it is this: God's will
must possess us entirely so that every bit of us is given over to

him. Then all the other things—the wonderful world of music, art, literature, human fellowship, politics, economics, and whatever—will take care of themselves, insofar as we are rightly aligned with his will. There is no possible way to be a Christian and give it just a little bit of time. God says, "Either/or." Even Saint Augustine had to confess, "I will, but I will not entirely."

Most people are really dilettantes when it comes to religion. They dabble in it a little bit, but they are never pierced through and through with the reality, the joy, the power, and the peace of the living God. We have few Elijahs today. When someone does rise up to remind us of the way of our salvation, of the extent of our creative opportunities, of the nature of the gospel, then it is so often the nature of the dilettantes and the unbelievers to join together to bring his work to naught. This was Jesus' observation: whenever a prophet arises, they crucify him or they stone him. Then the following generation hails him as a hero. They raise monuments to him and say, "Our great Martin Luther" and "Our great John Wesley." But when God raises up prophets who in their own day proclaim without fear or favor the full gospel, people cringe and begin to hide from it or conspire against it.

We can see the human tendency to bring God's work to naught in many fields of endeavor. Take for example the field of medicine in regard to that once dread disease, poliomyelitis. Sister Kenny, a nurse in Australia, worked out a system of massage and exercise that proved effective in curbing the effects of paralysis in many cases she treated. Instead of accepting her findings as a boon, the medical profession brushed her off. Later along came Salk, with his marvelous discovery of antipolio vaccine. What did he get? Acclaim from the medical profession? No; opposition. We could examine the history of development in many fields. Rembrandt, Bach, anyone who comes along with something marvelous and new—what do they get? Appreciation? Understanding? No; controversy, distortion, trouble are what they get. But they get something else. They get a tremendous joy, for even in the suffering of failure and misunderstanding they know reality. They see it and are unafraid.

II

How is it possible that some of the most ardently "religious" people, who are far from dilettantes, can not only make of no effect what has been done, but even go contrary to the will of God? It is important to see that religion is not good in itself. Religion is our response to God. Revelation is God's coming and letting himself be known.

Our religions are only as good as we are, in the sense that they are always the expression of our interpretations, which are mixed with our fears, our finitudes, our shortcomings. Therefore we manufacture a kind of status quo religion wherever we live; one that does not break too radically with the ordinary. Then we worship God and say, "O Lord God, we bow down, we give, we worship. But, O Lord God, stay within these confines of our acculturated, status quo religion." And God replies, as he revealed his word to Amos, "I hate your worship; it is a stench in my nostrils," because the acceptance of the status quo is always original sin. Is that not right? The acceptance of the status quo simply means that we say, "What is, is right"; but we know that what is, is not right.

We know that God needs to remake us inwardly and God needs to remake his world. Otherwise we will keep having the corruption, the destruction, and the trouble that is coming upon us. We know that we need a fuller, truer, more piercing, more demanding, and more real religion. Human efforts are insufficient; therefore it is time for God to act.

"It is time for the Lord to act." But it is up to us not to pay undue attention to our guilt feelings, which only make it worse and worse for us insofar as we cater to them. We must let God remove our guilt feelings when he acts in us to deliver his people.

How does God act? First of all, someone will say immediately, God certainly doesn't interfere in human history, does he? You aren't proposing to tell us that God manipulates things, that God comes in and *does* things?

I remember writing an article for the Fellowship of Reconciliation, in which I was pointing out a few things that had happened in human history. I said that God was ultimately responsible for the good that happened. After I sent the article in, I got it back by return mail. The editor said, in effect, "Don't be ridiculous. Don't give God credit for what human beings have done. It is ridiculous that God should act in human history."

III

Unless, however, it is God who acts through us, there is no conclusive, stable, creative, finally sufficient action in human history. God and God alone is the center of reality. Only insofar as we win the victory that comes in terms of being rightly aligned and rightly related and having the power inside and outside—eternals taking charge of both externals and internals—do we have the victory.

Yes, I believe that God takes the sovereign initiative. God is the one who ultimately elects his people. We have moved away from all doctrines of election or predestination. Predestination and election do not mean that God overrides our freedom, that God does not need our freedom. These doctrines mean—or should mean—that ultimately history is a confluence of God's will with human will, but he always has the sovereign initiative. In one sense, God can just let history go its own way, letting the consequences of our choices accumulate. That is all he needs to do in order for us to destroy ourselves, because that is the way we are headed and that is the way we are structured in our affections. We think mostly of ourselves and of our ingroup. But God has created us for a purpose, and therefore he does not only let our choices and their consequences go on in their natural way, but he also injects into history his sovereign purpose, trying all the while to change it and to woo us into different ways of choosing.

God is, so to speak, like a cybernetic mechanism—if we may permit a poor illustration. When a torpedo of this nature is fired at a ship, the ship's captain will try to change course to avoid being hit, but under automation the torpedo by its feedback system will alter its course and find the ship. So we try, like Jonahs, to dodge God's ways. We try to get away, but God is always there, meeting us in his way. How different if we

would meet him in a positive, constructive way! I wish we
would set our way toward his way, and instead of his always having to chase us, so to speak, he would find us coming toward
him.

IV

God guides the world in this way. It is therefore time for God
to act. He acts in history generally; he acts in terms of the consequences of our choices and our human responsibility; but more
than that he acts in terms of his sovereign initiative.

In what ways does God act more specifically? God acts
through prophets whom he raises up. There never was a critical
time in human history when God did not send his prophets to
deliver his people. Whether or not history is delivered depends
upon the response it makes to the prophets. Always the people
perish without vision, but God sends his vision to the prophets if
they will only heed and hear.

God also acts through martyrs. There never can be any salvation in human history apart from suffering. Lonely is the way of
the prophet. He who stands at the center of history had to know
rejection—not only persecution and misunderstanding and being forsaken, but final rejection and death at the hands of
man. This has been the history of humanity. It has never been an
easy task. It is always the hardest task on earth to persevere, doing nothing but God's will, hoping and wishing and praying for
nothing but God's will.

God always has his martyrs. This generation has seen so many
martyrs, so many self-giving people who have died. So much
blood has been shed because people have genuinely believed.
God is still raising up his martyrs. He raises up statesmen and
artists and writers, and most of all, he raises up his faithful congregation, the living stones of his great building, where every
stone counts, where every living part is important. For this reason there is not one person who cannot help in a wonderful way,
under God, to make a new human history.

God has shifted the gears of history, accelerating us into a
new speed. I am convinced that we now stand at the point of ei-

ther accepting a whole new way of life, in terms of the open, inclusive, and concerned community, or else we must face the consequences of not going at God's pace and God's time. Either we are going to destruction or else we are coming into a new age.

Now I personally, in my own inner spirit, am expecting and awaiting God's new age. I feel in my heart and know that I cannot deny that God has called me to proclaim the new age of the Spirit. God says to us, "You need not perish. Turn your ways to me and you shall live."

"It is time for the Lord to act." It is time for the Lord to act and he is willing. He is ready. History in one respect is like a ferris wheel. When the ferris wheel stops, if you want to get off, you may do so. But if you don't get off, the wheel turns on. Some people think that any time is the time for salvation. That is not so; that is pure sentimentalism. There is such a thing as reaping what we have sowed, when the sickle must be put to the harvest. And there is no such thing as escaping the consequence of our guilt and sin when we fail our chance. I believe that the ferris wheel has just now come to the point where it is time for us to get off. This is the time for God to act.

This is the deepest prayer of my life: "I don't understand history. I don't understand my own life. But I do believe that thou art God, a living God who acts. If I leave my life completely in thy hands, I will be used." In answer to this prayer there will come a new age for our children and our children's children, who, whatever the nature of that truth, will rise up to call us blessed. But in calling us blessed, they will not only honor our generation, they will praise him who, in this generation, acted.

10.

When the End Comes

The prophets prophesy falsely, and the priests rule at their direction; my people love to have it so, but what will you do when the end comes? Jeremiah 5:31.

THE WORLD SEEMS SET on its steady course of corruption, and even possibly destruction, while the church seems helpless to change it. Two thousand years of Christian preaching and influence, yet here we are. While decay spreads like dry rot in both civil and public life, ministers in the pulpit drone nursery rhymes and croon lullabies. Both soft-spoken liberalism and fiery fundamentalism have failed the church and the world. Why? Jeremiah tells us the truth.

I

"The prophets prophesy falsely." The prophets today are the theological leaders who set themselves up to speak for God. True prophecy always proclaims the gospel that God is able to deliver his people both from their personal sinfulness and from the power of evil in high places. God can help if we but will. Never will he violate our freedom even to destroy ourselves, but as the Bible says, he wants all to be saved and come to the knowledge of the truth (1 Tim. 2:3–4).

True prophecy is the proclaiming of the good news of repentance and reformation. The Kingdom of God is at hand. It is up to us to repent and to believe the gospel. The true prophets center their message in the faith, hope, and love which are of God and in the victory which overcomes the world. Genuine preaching calls men to let God reorient and remotivate them within his inclusive community of concern, knowing that it shall be done to all according to their faith.

False prophecy majors in the general sinfulness of men which becomes the excuse for even the believer to stay as he is. It holds out forgiveness and acceptance to people as they are. It offers what Bonhoeffer called "cheap grace." False prophecy hails as Christian realism the secular scientific analysis of society, in terms of which the best that can be done is to balance power against power, thus selling the world out to constant evil. To be sure, such description is true of the world we actually know, but it is not the world that can be if we accept the will of God and trust him to leaven the whole lump of human behavior. False prophets scorn the promises of God as idealism. Therefore their false prophecy amounts to the gospel of an alleged realism. Accept yourself and your actual world, accept God's forgiveness, and merely do what you can within the rough-and-tumble of a world that cannot be changed. Even the old liberals were more demanding than that, both in personal and in social life!

Oppositely, fiery fundamentalism cries for the atoning blood of the Lamb and heralds his Second Coming. In the meantime the world must get worse and worse. Social responsibility and hope are "liberal" fancies and not the stern truth of the catastrophic end of the world. "Save your soul by confessing the only Son of God as your Savior," sounds the gospel message, "and don't get mired in the quicksands of worldly affairs." False prophecy of this kind never reaches the heart of personal and communal reorientation and remotivation within the open and inclusive community of the new creatures in Christ, those matured within the realisms of the love of God.

Some false prophets of our day even deny the God who acts in history. They substitute some Ground of Being for the Living God who holds the world in his hand, for judgment or for salvation. Thus prophecy for them is the description of the constant

conflict between the demonic and the divine influences which
are open to man. The Christian faith, however, holds out the
high hope that if men will but accept the will of God, both their
lives and their history can be radically changed. Besides, these
false prophets limit the promises of God to this life and thus
mock the greatness of God who only begins his work of creation
and salvation on this side of the grave. The Christian faith
stands or falls with the reality of eternal salvation. The true
prophet knows that God is not the God of the dead but of the
living, for unto him all live (Luke 20:38).

II

"The prophets prophesy falsely; the priests rule at their direction." Monsignor Knox even translates the line freely as
"priests that clap their hands in applause." * Why do the priests
uphold false prophecy?

The priests, our ministers, are trained that way in seminary.
The theological seminaries are all too much the bottlenecks of
the Kingdom of God. Most seminary professors dread the fullness of the gospel. They have grown sleek and meek in the service of the status quo. Many of them have ulcers from working
too hard at conformity. They want to be accepted and belong.
They want to read, to cite, and to promote the proper authorities, who are, all too generally, the false prophets.

Unless I believed strongly in theological education I should
not have spent most of my life in a seminary nor work so hard to
promote such education. But I realize that much if not most
of theological education is misdirected and is following false
prophecy. That is why we need the true gospel taught all the
more. Seminaries, however, tend to teach their students, not the
high and holy demands for repentance and newness of life, but
all the sophisticated reasons why life and this world cannot be
changed. They tend to substitute words of man's wisdom for the
promises of God which demand the faith that is foolishness to
the world.

* *The Holy Bible,* tr. Ronald Knox (New York: Sheed & Ward, Inc., 1954).

In the same way our presses and periodicals become secularized. They join the false prophets in the acculturation of the gospel, thus killing its power. The periodicals grind out status quo thinking week after week and month after month, those which are avowedly "religious" as well as those that carry a section on religion. When a periodical like *Time*, for instance, highlights a religious leader as newsworthy, it is usually one who approves of our military involvement or our capitalist economy. Christian thinkers who dare to search the underlying motives of the secular world and call for a realistic reappraisal of our policies in line with God's will are usually ignored or dismissed with sophisticated condescension. To be sure, the way-out-peculiars are played up as exhibitions of the religiously bizarre, for the amusement and babbling of the unbelievers. Thus our ministers are brainwashed week after week to prefer status quo politics to any expression that approximates God's inclusive, cooperative way with the world. Thus in both faith and practical viewpoints, our priests are trained in and out of seminary to uphold the false prophecy of status quo theologians, the worldly wise who know not the radical power of God to change lives and the world.

To be sure, the whole climate of culture indoctrinates them not to believe the gospel but to accept the cultural, educational context through which they interpret and adjust themselves to the world. Ministers are mostly children of their world and of their times, not God's messengers full of power to judge and to help change the world. Then can they be called guilty? Yes, they share the guilt of the false prophets, because all of them at some time in their lives have available to them the true prophets who come with the cheer and challenge of the gospel message. They have in them God's image, God's call to new creaturehood and the new age. They feel stirred at the depths of their lives. But they look at the hardship of the true way. They sense the unpopularity of true prophecy. They remember that the true prophets of God have been stoned and crucified, or in our own day ignored or dismissed with faint praise, not even taken seriously. Self-protectively, they remember the fleshpots of Egypt and wish to return there or at least, rationalizing their situation, they adjust themselves to where they are.

Those who dare persist in the gospel often find the gospel promise true that they shall meet persecution. Some suffer under it patiently and long. Some who dare to declare their opposition to segregation, for instance, even in the spirit of saints, have lost their pulpits. Some who have dared to question bureaucracy in the seminaries have lost their positions. Some high-minded but low-spirited ministers quit the ministry. To be a true prophet of God in a modern church, or in any church at any time, is not easy. But most ministers become priests who rule at the direction of the false prophets. Out of insecurity and guilt they even clap their hands in applause.

III

Why is this? Because the "people love to have it so." Who creates the false prophets? God? Of course not! The evil of their own hearts? Only as the occasion for their letting themselves become false prophets. They prophesy mostly to please the ministers, the priests, who mostly want to please the people. And the people love to have it so. There's the rub.

Religion is man's response to God. Man fears and hates God because God always threatens the status quo. God says: repent or perish. Reform or face corruption and destruction. We people do not want to repent. We hate to reform. We are too tired and burdened as it is. Life is too complex; it is too demanding just to keep living.

For this reason we make our response to God—our religion—a hiding place from him, respectable enough to make us feel that we are worshiping him, but never good enough to persuade us that we are really trusting and obeying him. Thus our religion represents the status quo. It is a rationalization of our actual half-hearted allegiance to our Maker. No wonder we dread and hate to have the true prophets rip the blindfold from our eyes and make us face the dazzling truth of our relation to God.

True prophecy involves full and right relations to God, the only way that life can be truly good and give satisfaction, but such a state of life and society seems but an impossible ideal, and we call anyone who proclaims true prophecy—God's power to change life and the world—an irresponsible idealist. Either we dismiss him as a harmless fanatic or fight him as a dangerous agitator.

Yes, people love to have it so. They admire and spoil the false prophets with praise. The people want to be right with culture. Perhaps we give lip service to a new day of a worldwide religion beyond nation and race, even beyond the ideologies of present religions, based on nothing but God's love for all men and our common acceptance of them, in creative, cooperative concern. But when it comes to the mature living and working of such faith into our common life on every level of responsibility, we prefer to echo the viewpoint of the newspapers and the State Department or the worldly-wise of our communities, rather than the sharp and decisive will of God for all people. The people of the churches prefer their comfortable doubts and fashionable denials to the painful duty of believing and letting the healing power of God change our inner and our outer lives.

"My people love to have it so." We prefer tranquilizers and sedatives, yes, even sleeping pills in religion, to the summons to awake and arise, to be counted on for the coming of God's kingdom. We want soothed consciences and smooth assurances that all will somehow be well even without repentance and newness of life. We pay our preachers of false prophecy well. So the false prophets, the priests, and the people all have their way. We are as we are; we keep going as churches, but without the prophetic power to change lives or to cure the ills of civilization. Thus it was, is, and seems to be, world without end.

IV

"But what will you do when the end comes?" Jeremiah's question demands an answer. What will you do?

What will you do when physical death comes? There is an end to life on earth. Life ends for us all. It is incredibly short and death hangs over us all. What if the Lord of life over death is not real because we have long listened to false prophecy and have hid from him?

In a Boston hotel I spent hours with a young seminary graduate who was about to conduct his first funeral. "All I can honestly say to the congregation," he told me, "is that now that the man is dead you had better forget about him and live while you have a chance; but that does not seem appropriate in a Christian church. What can I say and still be honest?"

If God does not fulfill our lives beyond this tiny breath, then he is not the God of the Christian faith. The full reality of resurrection we cannot know this side of death, but the Christian faith is the faith that death has been conquered, for from the beginning God has made it a door to the larger life. The one who really believes and lives such faith nothing can conquer. As Shakespeare put it:

> So shalt thou feed on Death, that feeds on men;
> And Death once dead, there's no more dying then.

But without such a hope, what will you do when the end comes?

Or what will you do when mental death settles upon you? Already our loss of meaning and hope is causing the collapse of mental health. If our cold war corruption and guilt overwhelm us further, what will you do? The end can be nearer for some of us than we think. During the Cuban crisis someone in California telephoned me in Boston in panic: "Is this the end?" I saw waitresses in an airport restaurant, white of face, refusing to be calmed. "They are going to blow up the world; what's the use of anything?" If further or deeper crises come upon us, have we the faith to keep sane or will our end come? Or if crises lead to catastrophe and we shall have to survive among ruins with infected bodies and death upon us, shall we have the health of life in God or shall we cry for the hills to fall upon us?

Can we stop the world from getting on its final collision track? If something remains, what will be the end? What will you do when the end comes?

Up to now we have been on comparatively pleasant grounds. Liberals have treated death as though only nothing or else good could await us. But as surely as God is a righteous God, we shall face our neglect and defiance of his way on the other side. Call it what you want. Names matter less than the reality. God will certainly have his way in the end, but "it is a terrible thing to fall into the hands of the living God," without defense. We must moralize the future life; liberal soft hopes are futilely false.

What will the end of life mean for you? What will you do when the end comes after death? How will you meet God?

Preaching is proclaiming the gospel, not primarily scolding or threatening. What, then, is the gospel? *God can change your life and he can use you to change the world.* You can lean on his promises and rest in his love. You can find the peace that passes understanding that the world can neither give nor take away, but only on the condition that you accept God as your only hope and his way as your straight path. This means living constantly in faith, in universal concern for the world.

When you do so, you can find the joy and peace in believing that the God of hope can give. Then you can rest in his will for time and eternity, and resting there, you can work to advantage in this world that needs your witness and your help.

"Behold, I set before you a blessing or a curse. Choose ye this day." * God can and will change your life and your world if you will let him be central and will accept all men creatively and with concern for his sake. Then you need not fear the end. Your end is God's good fulfillment of life in Love's eternity.

"The prophets prophesy falsely; the priests rule at their direction; my people love to have it so, but what will you do when the end comes?"

* Deut. 11:26; 30:19; Josh. 24:15.

PART II
Old and New

11.

The Age of Unimunity

> *Then said Hezekiah to Isaiah, "The word of the Lord which you have spoken is good." For he thought, "There will be peace and security in my days."* Isaiah 39:8.

KING HEZEKIAH had entertained messengers from mighty Babylon to whom he had proudly shown his riches and his fortifications. "What strutting foolishness!" erupts the prophet. "These riches will all be taken to Babylon and your sons carried as slaves to serve as eunuchs in the monarch's court." "That's good," thought Hezekiah, "for there will be peace and security in my days."

To some that is all that matters—what happens to me, what happens in my day.

King Hezekiah's response to the prophet is matched by that of a famous fundamentalist preacher who, vividly describing to his hearers the seven stages in the coming of Christ according to the Book of Revelation, each stage bringing increased disaster to the doomed, whispered to himself after each declaration of disaster, as he patted himself reassuringly on the chest, "*I'm* saved, thank God." One easily recalls in this instance the wisdom of the Buddha who observed that no one is so selfish as he who is first of all concerned with his own salvation. There are many who want peace and security for themselves in their own day.

In contrast to the attitude displayed by Hezekiah and the fun-

damentalist preacher, we have the statement of a young soldier
in Vietnam who, while deploring the war, thanked God that if it
had to come, it came in his generation when he could take his
share of suffering and sorrow.

I

Our topic is unimunity—the age of unimunity. This concept
goes deeper than the mere contrast between selfishness and selflessness, or between individualism and collectivism. It discards
and makes obsolescent the opposing of self-love and other-love.
Unimunity makes superficial the posing of unity against community or union against communion. In theological circles we
have contrasted *agape* as the Godlike New Testament kind of
love and *eros* as self-seeking. Our very modes of thinking have
been saturated with such contrasts, and our inner selves have
been torn between an impossible ideal and an oppressive actual.

To a large extent the West has lived on substance thinking,
cherishing the value of the individual and glorifying ego-involvement by calling it self-realization. Or, oppositely, it has
tried guiltily to put up selflessness as the truest goal of life. The
East all too often has accepted the losing of the self, whether release comes from the mere destruction of ego-involvement or beyond that from finding satisfaction through losing the self in the
whole or identifying the self with the whole. But neither West
nor East has succeeded even in formulating the releasing formula. Only unimunity can be the answer that is the realism of
reality.

What is unimunity? How can we go beyond this agelong dilemma between the self and the other, or between man and
God? How can we leave behind Hezekiah's satisfaction with
peace and security in his day, on the one hand, and the forced
losing of the self, on the other? How can we be rid of the drives
of the self, both for and from itself, without getting rid of the
self? How can we go beyond the unity which forfeits the self
and the community which is either a congregate of selves, still
driving, or a collection of selves running away from themselves?
How can we go beyond both selfishness and selflessness?

Unimunity, a term I have made up from "unity" and "community," has full unity and more. Its unity is perfect identity. Ultimately, in one dimension all reality is one. All there is, is of the one Spirit. Creation no more stands out from God than it stands in God. All existence is not only from God but in God. This identity, the principle and power of full unity, is the truth of pantheism, and that far it is genuinely true. God is multidimensional, to be sure, but in the originating dimension of creation God is congruent with, identical with, the same as, all things. Tillich was more right in calling God the "Ground of Being" than in calling him "Being itself."

Unimunity, moreover, is also the greatest possible power for distinction, for true self-being. For God as Spirit is also Love, and the nature of love is to be concerned for the other, to give him freedom, to give him the fullest possible opportunity to become and to enjoy his best self. All distinction is real as the purposeful creation of the Spirit who is Love. God works constantly for the fullest and richest possible differentiation not only for unity but for "munity," not only for oneness but for manyness, and for each one of the many as well as for the all together.

Therefore God and the creatures, whether of nature or history, are one, fully identical at their base, and at the same time distinct entities, real and significant. Unimunity involves, then, neither supernatural otherworldliness nor naturalistic secularism "without God and hope in the world," but full unity with the richest possible proliferation of difference. But distinction never becomes invidious; freedom never becomes unconcerned; self-improvement never becomes irresponsible. God is fully in, and yet more than, the world; he is more than, yet in and fully for, the world. And man is fully in God and God in man, and therefore man is all the more himself and all the more in, with, and for all others.

Unimunity knows full stress on self-acceptance and group acceptance without spurious self-love or ingroupism. The self and the group and all are the same, in one dimension, and can never become themselves until the full corporate reality becomes mature, fully developed, richly realized. The proper self includes the full potential self. Nor can the whole, the identical, become fully expressed, being love, until the spirit in each person and in every community is expressed as fully, as creatively, as differentiatingly as possible. Thus there can be no true self-love that is not other-love, by the very nature of things; and no true other-love that does not intrinsically and unconditionally express self-love and group-love. Unimunity is beyond both and yet fulfills both.

Christian *agape* is not selflessness. Here Anders Nygren * is wrong, disastrously wrong. *Agape* and *eros* must be seen in a new and fuller light. Unimunity is equally far from selfishness— the pushing of self—and from selflessness—the running from self.

Unimunity is self-fullness, which is the love of self within the love of God for all. Such love cannot but be totally for the whole community, yet neither as individualism nor as collectivism, but as a full member, where to love self is to love all and to love all is to love self. Apart from the reality of unimunity we cannot even think self-love, for it becomes a rationalization in some form or other. Unimunity, based on the power of the identity of the one in the many, and on the distinction of the many in the One, goes beyond the distinction between self-love and other-love, and alone makes possible the age of universal man. Man can become universal only within the reality of the universal community which can be constituted only by the full presence and power of God as Spirit-Love. Such a goal for human life is unimunity.

Each person needs to express himself. Each person needs to be fully important, fully expressed. God meant him to be. Hezekiah was altogether natural in his self-concern. In unimunity, however, a person is fully interested at the same time both in his own self and work and in all others and in their work, up to the limit of relevance. Only when God reigns supreme in his Spirit of Love can this happen. Then all men and all nations will bring their glory into the kingdom. God speed the day of unimunity! Nothing less is adequate as an ideal and power for the new age to come.

* Anders Nygren, *Agape and Eros* (Philadelphia: The Westminster Press, 1953).

II

Unimunity, then, means that no man is an island—the citation from John Donne that has by now become a byword—or biblically, that no one lives to himself and no one dies to himself (Rom. 14:7, 8). Each person and each group is free to try to do so, and we do try. But by so doing, we deny our own nature. We fail because we deny God's purpose for us in creation, which is inviolate in character. Apart from God's purpose in creation for us we cannot be satisfied. Thus each person needs to become truly himself—a genuine distinction—but he cannot be himself unless he realizes that he must also be at one with all others.

This is the reason that no attainment pleases long and well if it is invidious, at the expense of others. This is the reason that we have to lose our lives to find them, which really means that we can find true fulfillment only in and with others. This is the reason for Whitehead's stressing so strongly that nothing can duly matter to us unless we are aware of and concerned with the consequences of our lives for others.

Whether we live and whether we die, we must live and we must die to the Lord. This is what King Hezekiah forgot. Creation as distinction is no fall of man. Only when man creates separation out of distinction is creation spoiled. Pluralism is no fault, history proliferates pluralism; only the pluralism that denies the ultimate unity, the ground of all in the one identity, God as Spirit, bedevils human history. In unimunity the more one we become in line with the Ground of our being, the more we become ourselves, the richer become all distinctions of creation.

In unimunity, furthermore, no one can live unto himself in the present alone. That is what Hezekiah forgot. He was concerned for his own day. Each generation lives from the past in the present toward the future, as one fabric within the creative purposes and providence of God. The Book of Hebrews says that "they," or previous generations, the ages and heroes of faith, cannot become perfect without us (Heb. 11:40). God is perfecting his work through the generations, and we owe what we are and have to the countless ages. Ingratitude at this point is not only culpable but is also immaturity, ignorance, thoughtlessness. The heroes of the past—no one in the past— can be perfected without our right response. God is one and all generations in God are one.

Time in God is only learning love, for eternity is God's time, and God is Love. If eternity is adjectival to God, eternity can mean only the living of Love, a reality that outruns time, which is for the learning of love. God is both temporal as concerned with pedagogical process and also beyond time as the living of love, where succession, in this sense of goal-seeking, is done away. When we come to mature manhood in unimunity, the communion of saints will be realized in God, but not until all generations have learned the life of love in him.

God's pedagogy goes on beyond time, as the learning of love, as the everliving and learning in love. To be real is to be in love. To be mature is to live in God, fully at one with all, past and present, and for one and all. Especially unimunity then points to the future. The future is God's call on all for all. The future is the radical reality of God's openness to all creative change and growth. Thus the past and present point to the future. The Bible says that they without us cannot be made perfect; they depend now upon the future.

And so do we. We shall soon be gathered with them, awaiting also the perfecting of the saints in the future. God's eternity is the fullness of his love for all to prepare for them the fullest opportunity to live and to learn in love. But long before eternity, time stretches long and real, the pedagogical process in which we ultimately are one. No generation lives unto itself. That is what King Hezekiah forgot.

As generations, whether we live or whether we die, we live and die in the Lord and for the Lord. Unimunity is the corporate oneness fulfilling each, where no one can be perfected without the all in God, and the all of creation cannot be perfected without the each one of creation. Therefore all creation waits for the perfecting of the sons of God, where even the Son and all sons must be subjected to God, in line with his love and in his love, that God may become all things to everyone.

Now look back on Hezekiah's attitude. Thank God there will be peace and security in my day! He was not only selfish, he was ignorant and foolish. There can be no peace and security in any day until we are willing to accept peace and security in all days. We live now for unimunity and in unimunity, as far as it is granted us; we live for the new, not only in human history, but in eternity. The promises and providences of God are transgenerational.

III

The new age must then be the Age of the Spirit. Apart from the Spirit the age cannot come to be. He is the rock of reality and the Source of significance. But the age will have definite marks of the Spirit.

One mark will be the creative fulfillment of race relations. We have lived in an age where motivation has been mostly color-bound. Few have been free in the spirit to transcend the problem in themselves and to be at their maximum best to overcome it. Now we are told to be color-blind. But that is like going from selfishness to selflessness. To be color-blind is to forfeit the rich differentiation of creation; it is to fail of unimunity. We must instead become color-rich. In the reality of the presence and power of the Spirit we must accept, to God's glory and to the glory of all races, the fact that we are different.

Distinction must not mean segregation; difference must not be divisive; nor must we ignore and make nothing of distinction. We must mature to the point where we can accept the distinction as enrichment, let races enjoy differentiation without cavil and embarrassment, but provide all opportunity both to become distinctive and to have all common privileges and responsibilities. We must go beyond being either color-bound or color-blind to becoming color-rich in race relations, here and all over the world.

Another mark of the Spirit is that we must also go beyond individualism and communism in property relations. We must go beyond both private enterprise and communal enterprise in the sense of rivals. The total community must no longer

be subservient, even in ideal terms, to the value of the individual and to individual or group freedom, nor must the
individual's rights be sacrificed for the good of the state. Unimunity fulfills the need of both private and communal enterprise
by full concern for the freedom and the security of each and
all. The technical outworking of such a reality will have to
become a creative enterprise among men and nations in the
new age of universal man. I have hinted at democratic socialism,
but words are flags that divide, and I know that the new will
have its own distinctive meaning and use of property. If we get
the reality of the relation of unimunity, we shall find the
wisdom to pioneer creatively for an age of abundance that
will not engender insecurity. Capitalism and communism in
any case are obsolescent and await the fulfilling constructive
revolution by unimunity of property relations.

The third mark of the Spirit is that unimunity will go beyond
both one-worldism and nationalism. We cannot rightly affirm
the nation without going on to world law and world reign, the
hegemony of nations under and in God. But neither can we
accept such a one world without putting even more stress
on love of particular nations and particular peoples. To become
one in unimunity is to glory in distinction. Everywhere there
must be more patriotism, not less. Each flag must become more
precious, not less. Each heritage must become more sacred,
not less.

No nation in unimunity can be itself without the common
good which is rooted in the very identity of reality. To become
patriotic passionately and insistently is to appreciate the distinctiveness of the nation which cannot be fully real and right except in line with the fullest acceptance and appreciation of all
nations, and of the common solutions in the age of universal
man.

But how can these things be? Be concrete. Begin by accepting
your full true self within the reality of unimunity. Know yourself,
accept yourself, experience genuine *metanoia*—the conversion
of the self which enlarges it to its full dimension. You become
your full, distinctive self, then, only by at the same time accept-

ing in increasing reality and enrichment the needs, problems, and resources for all men.

By so knowing and accepting yourself you understand your primary reality to be in the presence and power of God, as your truest self, first by creation, and then by mature understanding and acceptance in freedom. Man cannot bring in the new age apart from God. Rather, then, make the sun rise! But neither can God bring in the age apart from man whose freedom he has made and whose distinctive life he respects and appreciates. God, then, is the final power for the new age of universal man, but man is the key to it. No one can measure what God can do through you if you let him work the fullness of his purpose in you.

So, living in unimunity, you will turn in thankfulness to appropriate your heritage. It is rich beyond your imagination. Don't live like one suffering from amnesia. Learn to know, to appreciate, and to accept your heritage. Remember that those who have gone on before you cannot be perfected without you. Don't commit the sin of Hezekiah—wanting peace and security for your day alone.

Finally, live fully for the future. The present is God's chance to remake the past and to create the future. The future is the radical reality of God's continuing creation. Repeat the past forward, live fully for today as you are focused for the future. The status quo always tempts you to original sin, the sin of accepting what is actual, rather than God's rich promises of what can be.

The age of unimunity is about to dawn. This is not rhetoric but reality. Dare God to open your eyes, to open your lives, and to make you the messengers of his love. Behold, I bring you tidings of great joy which shall be to all people.

PART III
New Testament

12.
Living Truth

... *as the truth is in Jesus.* Ephesians 4:21.

THE PROBLEM OF PREACHING to the new generation is that there is a growing distrust of truth. There is confusion, yes, but confusion can be cleared up. Ignorance can be conquered. Even apathy can be overcome. But we face today a maniacal mood of nihilism. We do not strangle meaning nor freeze motivation; we abandon both. Faith at its basis is affirmation of meaning. Modern man, now in the United States, trailing Europe, abandons all faith, not as a deliberate choice even, but as a letting go of the meaning of life itself, and surely of all theories to account for life or to direct it.

Jung claims that Western culture is finally discarding the protoimage of Christ as central to its meaning. The overarching meaning of the centuries is dissolving at the deepest level of the racial unconscious. Tillich in his profound chapter in the *Festschrift* to Jung wonders and worries whether symbols ever reach permanent reality or whether they are created by the needs of an age, only to perish with the ending of that age.

Is the stupefying lassitude characterizing distrust of truth in our generation the notification of the ending of the age of Christ, or is it, rather, the outcome of guilt and dread? Do we feel so guilty for our barbarous cult of killing, the baring of man's beastly conduct from German gas ovens to our own Hiroshimas and Vietnams, and so fearful of the future with its sudden common dying or its even worse woes of tortured living, that the mind blanks out at any challenge of faith? Surely pious protestations of Christ as the truth seem hollow mockery of man's hopes. In any case, nihilism is upon us as a wet blanket over feebly burning coals.

And yet within such weary absence of faith and such tempting vacuity of meaninglessness, Christian leaders seem to hasten for final refuge to the one name not guilty of acculturation nor besmirched with the holy hypocrisy of Christian history. A genuine life, uttering simple stories, becomes the master model of all who believe that not all history has run aground in nihilistic relativism and not all truth has disintegrated within common guilt and dread.

All Christian confessions claim the love of Jesus. The fundamentalists flee their name and, renaming themselves evangelicals, protest the center of their faith to be, not Bible or creed, but Christ as love. The neoorthodox, bemoaning their slippage, still cling to the centrality of Christ, and increasingly as love. The demythologizers stake their claim on the existential import of God's act once for all in Christ and the meaning for life of the myths that center in the Cross. The Tillichians find in the picture of Christ the very coming together of essence and existence. The death-of-God theologians surrender God and Christian doctrine but bring all that is radical to focus in Jesus and his love. The radical futurists, like Harvey Cox, who will not commit themselves to what may remain in theology, venture the very openness of the future in some terms expressible by the meaning of Christ, the "Man for others." From right to left and from left to right, clear across the board, whatever basis there is left for preaching seems to be "as the truth is in Jesus."

Today I want to suggest a master model in these terms that will be as fresh and as open to the future as it is needful for all times and for all conditions of men. I myself have been converted three times: once to traditional Christianity (I outgrew that conversion); then, in utter despair in my college days, to sheer honesty whatever the cost; and finally to the faith that I shall recommend to you today. I cannot find a faith more open than this one, more ready to be flexible; yet it is directive and definitive as a way of walking.

I

The truth in Jesus is, first of all, the truth of life. Jesus was an existentialist starting in the midst of life. Saint Paul and others made a theology of his life and teachings. Gautama Buddha similarly was an existentialist, albeit Buddhist thinkers have made a religion out of his living way. Socrates, too, was an existentialist, although Plato and Aristotle made philosophies out of his living truth. The truth as it is in Jesus is truth for life, for the living of it. There can be no trustworthy truth that is not first of all a facing up to life. Faith's first affirmation is the acceptance of life itself. To live is to believe, to affirm at least that life is worth living, going on, rather than escaping in psychosis, in incapacitating physical illness, or in suicide. Whoever accepts life has faith; faith as the acceptance of life, furthermore, involves the acceptance of some meaning.

But what meaning? Youth especially are chary and wary of all theory. They rebel against absolutes. For them doctrines mean death. Over and over again I hear them chant, "I believe only what I feel. I want to be a useful animal, living, working, just being myself, rather than any phony philosopher or hypocritical believer." What they are saying in fact is that truth cannot be trusted. There is no such thing as truth, they clamor, apart from the concrete life we know, the life we know by living. Only living truth will do.

The truth as it is in Jesus is living truth. It is for life. If truth finally is not living, for life, for the living of it, it is not worth having. Jesus is the way, the truth, and the life precisely because the truth in him is, first of all, not in a book, a theory, a doctrine, but a way of life. "I am the way, the truth, and the life" (John 14:6). Truth must always come right smack in the middle between way and life. It is dynamic, moving, on the way to life. We have not a premade life but we make life by the way we respond to living truth. We create life as we discover the meaning that can be lived.

Jesus' whole life spoke for authentic existence. The Sermon on the Mount, the parables, his temptations, and, finally, his death were in the interest of a kind of life. He defied the encrusted status quo; he decried man's subservience to law; he broke even the most sacred laws of the Sabbath in order to heal and to help. A New Testament writer summarized Jesus' mission as one to bring life, and life in its fullness (John 10:10).

If we want truth as it is in Jesus, we must find it in life. And whatever faith we affirm spurns the truth as it is in Jesus unless it continually brings every affirmation, every assertion, every directive, to the test of life. Truth at its heart must be living, and no God can be worshiped, served, or loved who is not the God of life and for life, the Living God. Whoever makes life both the first and the final test cannot accept any truth but living truth.

II

As the truth is in Jesus, the truth is also concern. Jesus, we have heard over and over, was "the Man for others." He made love central to his life and teachings, the full love of unlimited forgiveness and constant for-ness. His was the life of universal for-ness. His was the God of love, whom he dared call Father. And his was a high, austere, nonsentimental love. The father of the Prodigal Son gave him his property far too early, we think, to waste and to abuse, and never went after him to call him back. He left the son alone to mature. And when the son matured and came back he was still *for* him and took him back without reproach. He welcomed him back with a feast of joy (Luke 15:11–24).

Concern is real only when it centers in the need of the other, and when we are willing to learn to know and to respect that need. Here in one formula we have the concrete directive for which the world is waiting: always and ever be completely *for* all people, for their best; and if you really are, you cannot help keeping your own self best for them, too. Thus the truth as it is in

Jesus is no abstract formula in the false sense of removing thought from life; it is the most concrete directive wedding thought to life.

This is the only formula I know that you can trust completely without becoming fanatical, for the more you live it, the more humble and forbearing you become. You learn to enter into the lives of others, seeking to understand and to minister to their needs. This formula permits no moralistic do-gooding nor escape into mere study or intention. The whole self is involved, whether for action or refraining from action as needed, on behalf of and as a member of the entire community. Here, then, is truth directly for life. Here is living truth. It is existential and more than existential, for the whole world of learning becomes important to help life and to focus on the needs of life.

A woman in Harlem stabbed Martin Luther King, believing him to be a Communist agitator. The knife was left in his body, right next to his heart. Now, Buddha was an existentialist. He said that if you find a man with an arrow sticking into him, you don't discuss the situation but you pull out the arrow. For three hours, however, the surgeons worked carefully and slowly to ease out that knife in Dr. King, after meticulous study of x-rays, for the slightest jerk on that knife would have caused it to break through the aorta and kill him. What was needed was not resolute, un-thinking action, but action in the service of concerned knowl-edge. This is why we have colleges and medical schools. This is the reason science perfects x-ray machines. We have to be exis-tentialists, if by that we mean taking needed action, but we have to take that action within the richest and fullest possible back-ground of knowledge. The truth as it is in Jesus is concerned truth in life, but needs the backing of careful training for life.

You may think that, as the truth is in Jesus, all we need to do is to love. The radical left in life and the radical left in theology all shout love. The death-of-God theologians all speak of love. But to make concern ultimate we must come to Ultimate Con-cern.

If love is final for life, the deepest meaning and reality of love must be living. If need is created by the world in which we live, and is life's attempt to be in proper functioning relation to that world, then the creation of that need reflects the nature of the world that created it. If man needs love at the center of his life, he needs to be related to the Love that is central to the world.

Modern young people revolt against all absolutes. Absolutes oppress life, they say, and offer false promises. We must live in relativities and be mature enough for such life. They are right, of course, for whoever has knowledge of God as love has no faith. Whoever has all the answers has no faith. What he has is knowledge. But from within a world like this we cannot have *knowledge* that God is love. We are finite and cannot know.

We have to accept on faith our ultimate presuppositions for living and thinking. An incomplete cosmic process, with the evidence not in, precludes knowledge. And we live in a world of hate and fear, of corruption and destruction, and, even worse, of a callous, habituated, smug hypocrisy of respectable people. These facts stack the evidence against God's being Concern, against God's being Love.

There is, however, much theoretical indication that God is Ultimate Concern, a claim bolstered as much by the breach of the good as by the living of it. I have devoted most of my life to demonstrating that God as Concern is a warranted faith. Finally, however, faith in God comes down to just that, the venture that what we most need can be had. Therefore our first need is to live the truth and only then to seek that fuller knowledge which in the field of religion corresponds to the medical school and the technology of the x-ray machine.

I think we are in for the greatest revolution in theology the world has ever seen if we try to take seriously the truth as it is in Jesus and make it, in fact, the universal truth for life, the living for-ness that is as concrete as daily bread and as comprehensive as the widest reaches of human knowledge, in all religions, in all secular knowledge, and in the avalanche of knowledge about to descend upon us. I invite you to the joy and to the pain of living that concern and to the ardor of carrying through that revolution in religious thinking which has to come if we are to enter the age of universal man, the age of universal for-ness.

III

As the truth is in Jesus, furthermore, it must be a truth of freedom. Jesus came to set men free. He lived to make men free in the truth. Jesus, or a follower, promised that we can know the truth and that the truth can set us free. An early interpreter said that only he who loves God can know that truth, for he who does not love God cannot know the truth as it is in Jesus, for God is love.* Thus all our points come together naturally and reinforcingly in man's true freedom. The world is revolting for freedom. The common people are claiming their right. Freedom of choice, yes, as represented by the vote. Our side of the cold war calls that kind of freedom the freedom of democracy. But man also needs the freedom to property, the freedom to participation in the ownership and in the regulation that more and more must control technological civilization. The world clamors for both inner and outer freedom. We must combine creatively the best in the two worlds.

Freedom for life needs the freedom of choice. We must not succumb to totalitarianism. We know enough of communism not to fall prey to its curbing of personal freedom. We want nothing of it. As the truth is in Jesus we want an open society. We need as never before to break through totalitarianism in all parts of the world.

Our own task, however, is to fight with freedom and for freedom the creeping totalitarianism of our own country. We need to break the insidious, subtle power of the police state as symbolized by the CIA and the FBI. We need to put to death the beguiling manipulations of our news media, where the medium transforms the message and massages us into fatal sleeping sickness. Files on every college graduate, records of every progressive assembly attended, threats to freedom as dire ultimately as concentration camps, not only a paralyzed body politic but also a drugged social life—these are real threats to freedom. We need to stand up for full freedom of choice: in thought, in speech, in assembly, and in appropriate action.

We need also freedom of life. We have to master the forms

* John 8:32, 42–47; 1 John 3:18–19; 4:6–21.

of modern power or they will master us. Communism and socialism are attempts at such mastery. To some extent they have
succeeded. They curb man's mastery over man, freeing all for
full security of job, of home, of helps to health. Man's freedom
must thus also be defined in terms of his freedom from the fate
that threatens him in an unplanned society of the technological
tomorrow.

There is real truth in freedom through common enterprise,
as there is real truth in our own claim that we need freedom of
personal choice. Full freedom includes them both, as Teilhard
de Chardin writes in *The Future of Man.** The West and the East
seek two needed goals. The West seeks complexification—personal freedom in an increasingly technological society; the East
seeks totalization—a way for all to live together for the common
good. We need both personal and communal freedom for the
future.

Freedom for the future can come only through the fuller
faith. Neither fragmenting existentialism nor absorption ideologies will do. The truth as it is in Jesus is the truth of freedom
for each and the freedom for all. Jesus was "the Man for others,"
but he was also the man for all, because he was the man from
God and for God. In him lived and taught that universal Word
which is complete and universal for-ness. The truth in life and for
life, the living truth, is the living in love which is the truth for
every human being, that he may be authentic, real, free; but it
is also the truth for all that they may be free together. They need
to be free from the power and oppression of the few; they need
to be free to use together and creatively all the resources of the
earth and of the planets; they need to be free together from
want in the midst of plenty, by the common control of popu-
lations; they need to be free from the fear of war, in a world
that is one in law and reign, with all possible freedom for all
regions and sections; they need to be free from the conflicts of
race, especially on some new worldwide scale; they need to be
free even from the divisions of religion which make men hate
and condemn each other.

* New York: Harper & Row, 1969.

Only the faith in universal for-ness can set men free in all these respects. Freedom must be rooted in reality, in the very warp and woof of the universe. God cannot be the living God of love if he is not the God who maximizes freedom, freedom from himself, setting the world free, letting it become of age, and freedom from all the drives to self and to limited loyalties that break man's spirit and sap his most creative drives.

We need freedom for the future. Only the God who exceeds in possibility any and every actuality can provide that freedom. The future must be the most open possible that we can find, the faith that is as much discovered as delivered, and as much created as inherited. We seek the absolute future of total freedom, which involves nothing less than the living freedom of creative concern, the freedom to know the truth and to find satisfaction within it. Such is the faith in the living God that comes from the truth as it is in Jesus.

At the University of Glasgow some time ago I offered the truth as it is in Jesus in terms of integrity and concern, the same living truth that I am offering here. I offered both faculty and students the life and teaching of Jesus as their master model. A model is neither literal nor nonliteral; yet it is directive for truth and not merely conventional. A model, as Ian Ramsey holds, can go beyond picturing to become a disclosure model. A scientist in the audience, however, stood up to challenge my use of a first-century model, my use of the life and teachings of Jesus.

"All models are relative," he said, "and last only a few years. No truth can ever be said to be permanent."

"Oh?" I said, "When did science first decide to have no integrity?"

"Why," he replied, "integrity we have to have always."

"Always?" I asked. "And at what point do scientists now propose to have no concern, no concern for truth and no concern for life?"

"Why," he said, "concern we always have to have."

"Always?" I asked. He sat down suddenly and kept very quiet!

You see, the truth as it is in Jesus, the truth of life, of
integrity of life, the truth of concern, and the truth of freedom
are for keeps. We need them always. As you go out into life,
you can trust this truth, for it is for life. As you pursue education you can trust this truth, for it makes education relevant
always, as well as fully significant in its search for the even
fuller truth for life.

Harvey Cox once chided me by saying, "Nels, you choose
truth; I'll choose relevance, and we'll see who gets further by
his choice." I choose neither, but both. The truth that matters
is always relevant, for it is the truth for life. But waves of
acceptance come and go. Don't be fooled by them.

When I was in Hawaii, the most famous beach boy, known
as the Rabbit, took me surf riding. I watched the foamy waves
and said to myself, "This is it." But he would not let the
outrigger go. He let wave after wave pass that frothed at its
mouth. Then there was seemingly no wave, but the whole
ocean seemed to heave. "Go!" he shouted, and before we knew
it we were lifted on the height of the waters and tobogganed
toward shore.

The fullest truth is deep. Don't be fooled by temporary
foam. Let your life be lifted on the ocean's rising of the living
love of God, and you will find that as the truth is in Jesus it
is both relevant and real.

God grant you all to be real in both life and knowledge,
beyond our present confusion and negativism, that you may
find the life that can fulfill.

13.

Prayer and the Modern Mood

Build yourselves up on your most holy faith; pray in the Holy Spirit. Jude 20.

PERHAPS BECAUSE I did not say grace publicly in a restaurant when I was taken there by a conservative trustee of an evangelical foundation, he told me the following story. He said that his sister, who was also a trustee of the foundation, had gone to hear one of the most prominent of the world's theologians. While in the city, she was fortunate enough to be invited to dinner where this theologian was also a guest. Halfway through the meal, the theologian turned to his host and said, "Thank you for not insulting my intelligence by saying grace. It insults my intelligence when people think that mumbling a few magic words makes the food different."

At about the same time, I was reading Leslie Weatherhead's comment in the British Methodist *Recorder* that he regretted deeply the time he had wasted on prayer, particularly on intercessory prayer. I was astonished, because what comes the closest to my own life is prayer. I believe so strongly in prayer from years of experience, from long years of suffering and finding God near, that I decided I had better reexamine the topic of prayer. Were pray-ers like Jesus, who prayed all night, or Paul, who prayed without ceasing, mistaken? Was Socrates mistaken when he said he could do nothing without consulting his "spirit"? Was Gandhi mistaken when he died, on his way to prayer?

I

Christian prayer presupposes faith in a living God, in a God who is a personal spirit, in God who acts in human history. This is obviously the fundamental affirmation. Today we all know it is very popular indeed for even a theologian no longer to believe in God, to say, "God is dead." But those of us who know God as altogether too much alive for us, have a hard time accepting this statement. We know this reality. We know what the Bible means when it says that he who would come to God must believe that God is, and that he is the rewarder of them who diligently seek him (Heb. 11:6). It is not so much prayer in which we trust as it is God. Surely prayer, for most of us, is not a matter of manipulating God. Prayer is certainly not a karmic reality. Christian prayer, as far as I can under-stand it, means the appropriation of the presence and the promises of God.

The first and most important thing we receive in Christian prayer is that he who eternally is, becomes real to us. We appropriate his presence. A new dimension enters into our life. Because we are in a new relationship, because we are in a right relationship, we can also enter into the promises and the privileges, not in such a way that our praying earns some merit before God, but rather that we now enter into the very core of reality.

The prayer of Muslim tradition was right: "O God, if I serve Thee for the fear of Hell, send me to Hell. If I serve Thee for the hope of Heaven, deprive me of Heaven. If I serve Thee for Thyself alone, give me of Thy fullness." Not until we have so entered into the reality of the One who is ultimately concerned with each and all, that we ourselves become partici-pants of this reality and this relationship, can we truly pray as Christians. Prayer, obviously, is the appropriation of the

presence and the promise of God, and certainly it is no in-
trusion.

II

People who have a deistic view of God think of a living
God who acts in human history as himself intruding in his
creation. But we do not live in a mechanical universe; we do not
live in a universe with closed causation. God no more inter-
feres in the universe when he participates in its processes
and when his purposes make a difference than we do when
we through our bodies are continually changing and altering
the universe. Our purposes make a difference in the actual
world; should not God's? Even as through our bodies the world
becomes accessible to us without interference, so he who is
the author of the universe, he who is what Teilhard de Chardin
calls "the within," is able within the depth of his reality to work
in the universe in which he is the basic and abiding purpose.
We can rely upon his answers to our prayers.

Christian prayer also presupposes a parent-child relationship,
wherein freedom is not frustrated, but fulfilled by God's giving
of his presence and his promises. I have often heard people say
against prayer, "God would not do for us what we ought to do
for ourselves." He surely ought not to! If he did that he would
be a bad father. God never does anything for us which we
ought to do for ourselves. Whenever God does something he
increases our freedom and increases our responsibility.

When I make it possible for my daughter to attend college,
and when I send her off, I help to increase her freedom intellectually, socially, and in terms of all the maturity which I
have coveted for her. If I did her assignments and wrote her
term papers—if I did the things which she ought to do for
herself—then indeed I would be a bad father. But when I
make it possible for her to increase her freedom and her responsibility, her maturity, then my deeds and even my presence, if I go to visit her, are a help and not a hindrance.
God never violates human personality in the giving of himself,

or in the giving of his gifts. God always increases our freedom and increases our responsibility, when we approach him in prayer.

III

Christian prayer presupposes not only a living God but a God who is, like Christ, concerned for the total good of all and each. That means that God needs our prayer. Most people take for granted that God does not need anything; but that presupposes that God is self-sufficient being, not that he is self-sufficient love. A self-sufficient being needs nothing external; it just is. But self-sufficient love needs the other person to love back and to respond. God is not a supreme being, God is Ultimate Concern, the ultimate Spirit.

Only a bad mother can forsake her child. The poorer mother she is, the less she needs her child. The better mother she is, the more she needs the love of her child. Need can thus be an expression of perfection as well as of deficiency. There can be mothering and smothering also, but that is needing in a false way, and God does not need in a false way. He needs us and our prayers because he is perfect love.

A good mother is the mother who just naturally relates herself, identifies herself with the child, and needs the proper response. If the proper response is for that child to do it herself—the "Please, Mother, I'd rather do it myself" of the television commercial—then the mother allows that, of course. The better the mother, the less she can forsake or abandon the child, the more she needs this love and this relationship. If God is ever going to become real to us it is only insofar as we realize that he in his love seeks us and needs us. Therefore we can enter into this relationship.

Practically every creative theologian has been a man of deep and profound prayer. I do not mean the pop theologians of today, but the people who moved history, such as Augustine and Anselm, Luther and Calvin, John Wesley and Peter Taylor Forsyth. They were men of deep and profound prayer.

Life's greatest and perhaps final lesson is to accept all, no

·matter what comes to us. Really to trust God is to be able to accept all. This is not easy. Then, having accepted all, we must believe that beyond our acceptance God is going to do something, so that at the same time we expect good things from God. The most important things happen in God's way. Therefore, even when there is what Kierkegaard called in *Fear and Trembling* "infinite resignation," or the giving up of ourselves in this way, it is not a matter of retreating from life, but rather a matter of opening ourselves to the fuller understanding and fuller acceptance of life itself. Then prayer becomes a total concern for all and each.

When we wake up in the morning we should lift our arms and hearts and thoughts and think about the whole world, its people, all its needs, all its religions. We should think, certainly, about the United Nations and the problems that our own nation and other nations are facing. We should pray for a world of peace and the genuine openness to know what to do to achieve it. We should pray for a new understanding of and resolution of race relations. We should pray for Catholic ecumenism every day, as well as for the World Council of Churches.

We should also pray that God will restrain evil. We should face with and in God's power the Ogpus, Gestapos, and CIAs; we should confront the industrial-military might that wastes our physical resources on war and repression and controls governments. We should oppose in prayer, in God's might, the evils of drugs, especially alcohol, organized crime, and, indeed, all manner of evil. We should pray for everything that concerns human beings. And then out of our love and concern we also have a right to come close in our prayers to our own children, to our own problems.

The Christian faith is never a matter of selflessness. Selflessness is as unchristian as selfishness. Selfishness means the pushing of self; self-promotion and self-protection stand in God's way. Selflessness is the running away from self and thereby running away from responsibility. But self-fulness is the Christian point of view, in which you accept the whole world, you accept all of God's promises, and then, within that, you accept yourself as part of God's creation. You accept your family, and all your closest concerns. Within this hopeful reality of his presence and of his promises, you let everything rest in his hands, and let yourself be used in his service. That, to my mind, is Christian prayer.

IV

Christian prayer presupposes above all else, as our text tells us, that we pray in the Holy Spirit. I am genuinely concerned when I pray not to tell God what is going to happen. I believe that if we understand who God is, God more prays through us than we pray ourselves. God is more the subject of prayer than I am, because we have a unity in the spirit and the bond of peace. I believe that fundamental reality is God the eternal Spirit, and that all of us have distinctive beings or distinctive spirits within this ultimate reality; but it is only insofar as we realize this fundamental meaning and acceptance of God's purpose that we can truly pray. Therefore our prayer lies not so much in our words as in the total way we respond to God, to be used in his service. Prayer is basically *participation in the will of God*. Often we do not know how to participate, but we shall be led into participation as we keep on seeking his will. The reality of prayer is the Spirit literally in us, coinherence.

Christian prayer, therefore, is praying in the Holy Spirit, and through the Spirit finding the freedom we need. Most people are not free souls. There is nothing in the world more exhilarating than being a free soul, a genuinely free soul. All of us start with a body. We experience life through it, we mature in it, but we have our problems with this body. We are not free because we are always dependent upon it to some extent. Then we develop our minds. In our minds it is very easy to become conformists to all the things we hear and read and say and do. We are thus not genuinely free in mind. Freedom comes only through the reality of the Spirit within whom we transcend both our bodily and mental limitations. Then we are able to be free souls, regardless of what the world says about us or does to us.

Some of my happiest moments in life have not been the moments when people have patted me on the back and said, "That is wonderful." Some of my happiest moments have been the times when I have had to go by myself and make decisions that I did not like at all, because I knew they would be costly. I have gone apart and prayed, and I have made the decision. I said, "This is going to be hard." Then the Spirit of God has flooded my soul and I have gone out and faced the problems. I have faced them in the spirit that I am a free soul. The only thing that matters is for me to know and to do the will of God—not to be unconcerned about other people, for I must listen to them and understand them—and finally, having made my decision that this is the will of God, to say, "Here I stand; I cannot do otherwise." Most of us would find a new freedom, would become new people if we realized that beyond the bodily limitations and beyond all the fears we have in terms of social acquiescence, is the reality of the Spirit that can transcend them all, set us free, and send us singing on our way.

V

I believe that God has a dynamic plan for each person. As soon as we mention a "plan for each person" something goes sour. We get a picture of prefabricated individuals, and that is wrong. Or we think of puppets. God has no plan like that for us. But God instead participates in our lives in a cybernetic or "feedback" way. When he makes possible for us different choices and still we do not understand and continue to make the wrong choices, he is there with new possibilities, ever new possibilities, luring us on, urging us on, and helping us if we are genuinely open to him. Life can be basically different, can be basically changed, when, within the will of God, we are willing to find not a prefabricated pattern, but God's own working with us, in us, and for us, insofar as we will increasingly follow the way in which he leads. Instead of fixed regulations, God gives us *flexible directives.*

I did my doctoral study with Alfred North Whitehead in his process philosophy. I took every course he offered at Harvard, and have always been deeply indebted to him. One thing he held in particular, a very specific doctrine of personal providence, the way God works in human history. Whitehead said many things that are right and true. But I believe that even beyond Alfred North Whitehead's view, there is an understanding of the infinite and ultimate way in which God can work in our lives if we let him. We face today the most critical hour of human history. Never before has mankind been in the situation in which we find ourselves now. Many of us would despair; many of our children realistically do despair deep down in their lives.

But I have come to believe, and advisedly, that for only the five in Sodom, God can yet save the world. By this I mean that if there are even a few who will align themselves thoroughly with the will of God, and be so open to his purposes that together they can become the leaven, we can yet move into new relationships—international, national, as well as social and personal—in every aspect of life. In order to do so we must, above all, find that community of the Spirit, that inner reality of our lives, which sets us free, in terms of which we can have the vision, and within which we can have the power to implement this vision for a new world.

If these have been merely words, I shall have failed in the sense of giving a stimulus. But if, by the grace of God, his presence and his promises can become so real to you and so important in your life that the miracle of his presence changes you and sets you on the way to becoming a new reality in the world, for the world that needs it so much, then my purpose is fulfilled. I believe in the reality of God's presence and promises; therefore I believe in prayer. Will you not "build yourselves up on your most holy faith"; in the depth of your life, find him, his presence, and his promises until your life makes a difference wherever you are, to your near ones, to your co-workers and to the world?

"Pray in the Holy Spirit," and this life will be yours.

14.

Freedom in the Truth

> *If you continue in my word, you are truly my disciples, and you will know the truth, and the truth will make you free.* John 8:31–32.

MODERN MAN SEEKS for meaning even more than for freedom, security, and order, let alone truth. Increasingly logotherapy (Viktor Frankl's term) is recognized as essential to counseling. Multitudes, however, no longer seek for meaning within the Christian faith, and many who do, crave what Pope Paul in his trip to India called "the wider ecumenism." Let us consider the answer of three major faiths to the problem of meaning. Modern man in his search for meaning asks, "Who am I?"

I

The Hindu faith, at its center, answers that man is the deceived, living in the land of shadows. Shelley caught this mood when he wrote, "We look before and after, / And sigh for what is not."* That is true of human experience. The pope himself used the Hindu prayer when he said, "From the unreal, lead us to the real." To the question, "Who am I?" the Hindu faith answers that man is the deceived, living in the land of shadows.

---

* Percy Bysshe Shelley, "To a Skylark."

The Buddhist, at least in the original tradition, replies: Man, as he is, is the sufferer, living in the land of pain. To live is to be selfish. To be selfish is to be miserable. Therefore it is better not to live; it is better to be delivered from existence. Man is tortured on the wheel of his own existence. He is driven and drawn to self-torture by his own desires. Man is the sufferer, living in the land of pain.

The Christian faith, answering the question, "Who am I?" replies that man, as he is, is a sinner living in the land of law. The Christian faith makes man not merely a victim of circumstance or self-drive, but makes man himself responsible in some way for the shadows and the suffering. The shadows and the suffering are somehow intrinsically involved with his own existence. He participates in the forces that create his own plight. Faithless and rebellious, man lives in a state of guilt, and living under the law, a law which he cannot fulfill or change, man lives in a land of bondage. Man was meant for good, but man is self-deceived and suffers from his own guilty conscience. Thus man is a sinner living in the land of law and therefore under a bondage he himself has helped create.

These, then, are the three fundamental answers to the question, "Who am I?" "Man is the deceived," says Hinduism, "living in the land of shadows." "Man," says Buddhism, "is a sufferer, living in the land of pain." "Man, as he is," says Christianity, "is a sinner, living in the land of law."

II

Modern man in his loneliness and lostness also asks for meaning beyond the self. He cries, "Am I alone, am I really alone? Is there meaning that includes others? Can I legitimately ever say, 'we', 'us', 'our'?"

Hinduism answers that, basically, man is fundamentally alone. Deed and consequence, *karma* and *samsara* are personal categories. We are not others. We may never live their lives. Social customs, *dharma*, are necessary for our living together. But our place in social life and duties goes back to what we ourselves deserve from our previous living, particularly in previous existences. Social life then is an external fortuitous product of individual deeds. Therefore, Hinduism says, man ultimately is alone, no part of others in the land of shadows.

Buddhism, at least in its main interpretation, replies that man suffers with others. There is consciousness of pain together in the land of suffering. Therefore there can be compassion, sympathy, fellow feeling, pity. Some Christians who have spent their lives in Buddhist lands say that Buddhism fundamentally never goes beyond fellow feeling and a sense of pity. We are all caught up in this suffering together, and we can see that others suffer with us, but this is more pity than fellow feeling and fellow suffering because there is no hope in it. There is no ultimate social feeling.

When I spoke at Harvard's Center for the Study of World Religions on the question of the relation of Christian faith to other religions, I mentioned the social category. A Buddhist monk from Ceylon came up afterward. The one thing he could not understand was my saying that man was not only an individual; man is also a *socius*. I had said that man in social relation is just as real as man in his individual capacity. This did not seem right to him. He said, "Why did you say so? How can you say so?" This seems to be a strong response from Buddhism. To the question, Is there meaning beyond the self? the Buddhist faith replies: Man ultimately is alone in the land of pain.

The Christian faith speaks up, saying that man is not alone. We all know John Donne's much-quoted line, "No man is an island." There is room for necessary community arrangement and for fellow human feelings. But there is more than that to Christian community. We are guilty together. We share responsibility. And beyond that, even, lies the common human nature apart from which man is not man at all. No human being is what he is apart from his fellow-man. We are even identical in one dimension in the Eternal Spirit. Therefore we must be forgiven together and freed from our guilt together. Man is not alone in the land of law. Man is not alone in the land of bondage. Saint Paul said God has made us to be one person in Christ— even as we already are one by creation within the one Spirit. It is hard for us to conceive of all of us as being "one person" as

we think of a person. God has made us to be one person, one
corporate reality, one in Christ. Jakob Boehme expresses it beau-
tifully: "God has made us for the one love which is Christ in us
all."

III

Meaning centers finally not in faith, however, but in truth. It
is not necessarily what we believe, it is only what we believe
when it is set upon the truth. Meaning centers in truth. What
does Hinduism say that truth ultimately is? Hinduism says "Tat
tvam asi." Man must find truth through identification. In Hinduism man never finds truth in himself. He finds it by finding out
what is the most essential in him and by identifying himself
with what is ultimately real. The truth of the Tat tvam asi is
saccidananda, or consciousness plus being and bliss. Man becomes fulfilled in the truth by personal identification, by reaching his essential self. But truth allows for no social meaning.
There is no intrinsic meaning at all in the land of the shadows.
The land of the shadows fundamentally is to be escaped. There
is no genuine work of God in nature and history in that sense. As
to distinctions within the essential, Hinduism differs, but is open
to many creative interpretations.

The Buddhist original tradition makes reply that truth is
Nirvana, be it neti neti, "Not this," a final suchness beyond all
knowing, or a literally being blown out of existence, as the light
of a candle. Nirvana, to simplify a complicated subject, comes
down to one of two things: either an ultimate agnosticism beyond the fourth state, or else nihilism, being blown up. Those
are the two basic choices. Man can escape the land of pain
by being no more, at least being no more in any predictable
sense of that which we now know. Nihilism and/or agnosticism
are therefore, to the Buddhist, man's best final answers. But
there is no social fulfillment, no intrinsic experience of the "we,"
and no meaning of the land of pain, no reason for doing anything
in this life or for this life.

The Christian faith speaks up to say that man is a sinner who
can be forgiven and who can find meaning in and with others

because he has a common Father, the eternal Spirit, the Ultimate Concern. Bishop Robinson, whose *Honest to God* startled
the Christian world, said even there that ultimately, whatever
the interpretation, reality had to be personal and had to be love.
In *The New Reformation?* * he declared that the fundamental
thing about the New Testament is Abba! Father!—to be able
to look to God and know that there is a purpose there. In London
after *The New Reformation?* was published, Robinson said that
he agreed with me in calling God "personal Spirit" rather than
spiritual Personality.

IV

You either believe that there is purpose in life, that there is
purpose in creation, or not. If you believe that there is purpose
in life, the simplest and most adequate way of looking at purpose obviously is in terms of some personal category. Impersonal
purpose in itself is never adequate to the fullest that we know.
God is not a *spiritual Personality* but a *personal Spirit*, and upon
that all Christian interpretation hangs. God is not a spiritual
Personality, he is not limited in a substance sense at all, but
he is the eternal, infinite, all-penetrating, all-working Spirit. Since
we have a Father we can be forgiven. Therefore sin is not a mean-
ingless category.

The following story made a great impression on me. When
I was giving the Earl Lectures in California, a minister happened
to tune in to the broadcast of one of the lectures. He had
studied in a liberal seminary, had gone off to war, lost his faith,
and now was pastor of a community church. This particular
evening he was driving around aimlessly trying to decide
whether to give up his ministry, not knowing what he believed,
not knowing what to do, desperate in unfaith. He was half listening to the radio in his car, and one phrase of my lecture
struck him, he reported to me later. The phrase was, "the forgiven man." He drove out into the desert and for hours that night
he wrestled with himself. Is there Someone who can forgive

* Philadelphia: The Westminster Press, 1965.

men? Finally, toward morning, he knew that he could be forgiven. He went back to his pulpit and entered upon a glorious ministry, because he came to realize that life is not only a matter of the feeling of guilt; there is also the possibility of knowing that we can be rid of this guilt because we have One whom we call Father, One who can and does forgive.

We have seen truth in this life and for this life in "the Man for others," as Bonhoeffer calls Jesus the Christ. We have seen it in One who taught us to call God "Father," One who taught us that God is Spirit, that God is Love. In this Christ, in this Man for others we see meaning, not only in this life, because the Father has so identified himself with the Son, but even in the land of shadows and in the land of suffering. In the land of shadows and in the land of suffering we see him. But more than that, he has so identified himself with us and given us of his Spirit and understanding that we can understand the meaning of the land of shadows and the land of suffering.

The land of shadows exists in order that we might be free. How could we possibly be free if we knew everything, if there were no ignorance? If we are ever going to mature and make moral choices there must be a land of shadows. Some of you think there might be too much shadow. The problem of evil is a crucial one. But viewing the land of shadows we understand that the shadows of ignorance exist in order that we might come to the light, through wrestling and through struggle.

The land of suffering, too, is only so constituted in order that we might learn from the consequences of our choices and come to know the kind of existence that alone is real; that we might come to know God's way rather than our own way. But this is only our side of it. On the other side is the need of God himself to come to us in his love in such a way that he does not violate our freedom, does not force our freedom, but offers himself for us when we are ready, in the frustration of our fears, to receive him.

God can do so only by the Cross. The meaning of the Cross is God's self-giving, Love's finding a way to offer himself at such points as we are ready. Therefore the meaning of the Christian faith is not only that in this life and for this life we have the

truth, but also that we can understand the very meaning of the
shadows and the suffering as we lift them up to God. When we
learn that freedom in the truth, we shall find the security of
faith with its inevitable counterpart of doubt and creative insecurity. He who does not have doubt and creative insecurity
can never grow. Of course, the more we see, the deeper our
problems become. Sometimes it is because of an excess of life
that we suffer when God comes to us with the vision of himself
and of his will. But we then come to understand more fully the
order that is created in and for freedom by the Ultimate Concern.

V

I have discussed these problems with as much integrity and
competence as I can command, in many parts of the world. I find
that fundamental to Hinduism is this understanding of man deceived in the land of shadows who can become identified,
escape disorder, and therefore find a worthy salvation in many
respects, but with no understanding of any illuminating light
coming to us in the land of shadows, in order to bring meaning
to the shadows. The same is true of Buddhism. Buddhism understands suffering—and how we need a religion today that
understands man's frustration and suffering and problems! Buddhism has a deep understanding of suffering. But it has no one
to come into the land of suffering itself. The Buddha identifies
himself with man to show him the way out, but not in such a way
as to illumine the meaning either of the suffering or of that love
that will not let us go.

Christ as Spirit and universal Love, showing us God, is truly
the way, the truth, and the life. Christ shows us the meaning
of life in the Man for others, "the crucified creator." That truth
we can have only as we walk in the way. Truth is no mere
theory. Truth is no mere knowledge to be learned. The Buddhists
rightly call it "truth-reality."

As a teacher and writer I value books. I would not do so if I
did not believe in truth. But fundamentally, when we have
learned everything we can from books and theory and discus-

sion, truth will never create in us the way of salvation, until
Christ becomes in us the hope of glory, until God's presence
quickens our spirit, and we know in our spirit that we are
children of God. Christ is the truth, but he is the truth *on the
way to life.* Ponder this relation: "I am the *way,* the *truth,* and
the *life.*" As we honestly and openly dare to reach out in all
fullness for life, we shall find that Christ is the secret to the
finding of it.

Nietzsche once said a remarkable thing. He said that the
trouble with Christians is that they think too niggardly of God.
They do not believe enough in the greatness and the goodness
of God. They have too small ideas even of man—a slave morality.
We need a humanly impossible faith, in order to stand on tip-
toe for God's mighty inbreaking into human history.

We stand today in the living choice between either a con-
tracted faith that cannot help us in our need or an expanding
faith that, as we grow in the understanding of the shadows
and the suffering, will show us that Christ as the universal love
of God is the only truth that can set us free. I pray with all my
heart that we may all hear the voice saying, "Here is the Way.
Walk ye in it."

15.

The Sermon on the Mount
for Today

Matthew 5, 6, 7

IN THE SERMON ON THE MOUNT preaching and teaching come
together conclusively. The *kerygma* is not authentic apart from
the *didache*. The life of Jesus receives content through his teachings. The spirit of Christ is spelled out in the Sermon on the
Mount. The Word of God, the *logos*, here turns into words of
teaching, the *lalia*. The *agape* of the Cross and the Resurrection,
the lived, the acted Love of God, in these teachings give directives for the living of God's love. The *kerygma* and the *didache*
thus come together in the Sermon on the Mount to provide the
gospel of God's love for both preaching and teaching. All the
strands of Jesus' teaching come together here, prophetic teaching
as well as parable and wisdom literature, to form the gospel of
God's love, offering not only directives for conduct but central
meaning and motivation for life itself, a veritable collection that
could serve, and perhaps did, as a catechism of the church.

I

The Sermon on the Mount divides into seven basic messages.
First, life centers not in doing—certainly not in thinking or

feeling—but in being. States of blessedness are states of the
spirit, states of being. Blessed are the poor and the pure in
spirit. Blessed are those who mourn or who are persecuted for
righteousness' sake. Such lives are salt and light for the world.
Such states of being, such spiritual conditions, cannot be hid.
They stand like a city on a hill, not like a lamp in a bushel basket.
The good tree bears good fruit and the bad tree, bad. Jesus
invites us first of all to be. He wants us to make the tree good.
There is no other way to spiritual reality and power.

II

But being is not enough! The good tree and the bad tree
both *are*. True spiritual being, however, is unto God (*coram deo*)
unconditionally. Only if thine eye be single shall the body be full
of light. No one ultimately can serve two masters. We either
hate or love God. Our heart is where our treasure is. We can have
treasure in heaven only when we are unto God unconditionally.
All giving must be unconditionally unto God, the left hand not
even knowing what the right hand is doing. Those who give in
the sight of men have their reward. Prayer must not be public
for notice and praise, but must be in the inner closet. God hears
in secret and answers openly. Fasting must be genuine, hid
from men. He who fasts must even try to cover up his fasting in
order that his act be unconditionally unto God. Only when the
tree is good can it bear good fruit. Only when the eye is single
can the body be full of light. Only when our total selves are
unconditionally unto God can we truly be and do the good.

When we are unconditionally unto God we are judged by the
perfection of God. Therefore we cannot judge others. When on
the contrary we are in and for the self we see our own faults
as very small and the failings of others as great out of all proportion. The speck in our own eye becomes a log in our neighbor's!
We become self-protecting and self-promoting. In the sight of
God, however, we are unconditionally judged and can find no
grounds for invidious comparison or for boasting. How sensitively
Saint Paul takes up this note in his justification by faith beyond
all merit of salvation. The heavenly Father is perfect in his un-

limited love. We are bid to be mature in that same love. If we let ourselves be forgiven and accept remission of our unpayable debt, we can be unconditionally unto God. We can be perfect in no other sense.

Unconditional being unto God rests in the kind of prayer that centers in God's name being hallowed and in his kingdom's coming on earth as in heaven. We are bidden to address the God of perfect love who lets his rain fall and his sun shine on both the just and the unjust as Father. For all our life of need, for daily bread, for forgiveness, for power to overcome temptation and evil, we must look to One who is in heaven, whose love is perfect. The ascription of that prayer, "for thine is the kingdom, the power and the glory forever," fits the prayer perfectly, in line with being unconditionally unto God.

III

Unconditional being unto God necessarily involves being unconditionally for our neighbor. Our relation to God cannot be apart from our relation to our fellow-men. Unless we forgive those who have sinned against us, we ourselves cannot be forgiven. Our state of being before God is no isolable existence. God is for the world, and to be unconditionally unto him entails being with him unconditionally for the world. God and the world belong together. His will must be done on earth as in heaven. If we go to offer gifts to God and remember someone who has something against us, we must first be reconciled to that human being before we can have our gift accepted at the altar. We may think that an offering to God, life's most sacred offering, can free us from the duty of supporting father or mother. But God and family belong together and, as Jesus says elsewhere, God will not accept even any *corban* (Matt. 15:3-9, KJV). Our duty is plain: unconditional being unto God involves unconditional being for our fellow-men.

Such unconditional being unto God and neighbor involves the full law of righteousness. For those who are unto God and man unconditionally there can be no divorce. The two persons by the very purpose of God's creation are one flesh. Adultery is no matter of extramarital relations but a breach of being. The unconditionally pure unto God cannot even think adultery. In such being, neither can there be false swearing. A man's word must be plain "yes" or "no"; anything outside or beyond that is evil. Unconditional being is the same as complete openness. It is being unconditionally unto God and man that lays the self open to persecution and rejection.

IV

Jesus is not saying that there should be no divorce. Where marriage fails there is lack of unconditional being on the part of two people who should be one flesh. For the hardness of man's heart Moses had to recommend the giving of bills of divorce. But not in the ethics of the Kingdom of God; such ethics are a matter of being, not only of eschatological being, or of some eventual aspiration, but of theological being, the being a new creature, the being born from above, where men are salt and light and leaven.

Therefore not one iota or dot can be removed from the law. The law is never abrogated or minimized. In the Sermon on the Mount the good news of God includes the fulfilling of the law, not as law but as love. To live unconditionally unto God is to be free not of the law, nor for the law, but in the law. The law of full righteousness is a narrow way that few take. Those who do so find life and freedom within it; those who do not, meet destruction and the consequences of their breaking the law. No one will get out from God's debtors' prison until he has paid the last penny. And this no one can ever do. There is really only one choice: to leave the broad way of destruction and to take the narrow way that leads to life.

V

Nor is such unconditional being unto God and man right unless it generates positive action. Love must engender giving to those who ask and forgiving those who need forgiveness. Unconditional love does not give away the outer garments only.

It strips self to help others. Naturally such love fulfills not
only the law of compulsion, walking the required mile, but the
law of concern, walking the next mile also. Love does not hate
the persecutor but prays genuinely for his welfare. We know
such being by its action. Being always externalizes itself in
action. To be is to do. The tree is known by its fruit. The tree that
bears no fruit is no good, and evil trees have to bear bad fruit.
The nature of the tree is known by its fruit. Thorns cannot bear
figs. Not he who says, "Lord, Lord," but he who does the will
of my Father who is in heaven . . .

VI

Our being is governed not by what we are but by who God is.
God does not love all indiscriminately as he is often accused of
doing. No, God loves inclusively. He loves all as each one has
need. He sends his sun on the just and on the unjust, but his
love takes account of the deeds of men. The narrow and the
broad way are not alike to God, only his unconditional concern
is the same for all men in whatever way they are.

We could not live unconditionally unto God unless we trusted
him, unless we believed him to be in full charge of all lives and
indeed of all creation. We must not be anxious, for God clothes
even the lilies of the field and feeds the birds of the air. Jesus
knew that the lilies wither and that the birds die, most of them
untimely deaths. His point is not that no harm can come to us, but
that God knows even the falling of a sparrow. Life and death
subserve his purposes, and God is completely to be trusted even
in such transient and precarious life as that of the grass and the
fowls of the air. Be not anxious, though you lose your hair and
cannot add an inch to the span of your life. Ask, rather, and
seek and knock, for your needs will be fulfilled in accordance
with what God considers to be your needs. Whereas the Gentiles
seek after earthly comfort and security, you must seek after the
Kingdom. Then all else will be added to you, for the Kingdom
itself is enough both in this life and in the life to come. Whatever else you may get is only added. Only when we live unconditionally unto God and to our fellow-man can we be rid of

anxiety. Then we are thankful for whatever comes, for each day
has its own measure of evil to face.

VII

Only such direct being unconditionally unto God and to men,
because God loves unconditionally and inclusively, can produce
true authority. Spiritual authority does not come from lording
it over others. It comes not from power. It comes only when
men hear the words of Jesus and do them. Those only hear the
words of Jesus and do them who live, as he did, unconditionally
unto God. Their lives are like the wise man who built his house
on the rock. All other kinds of living are building on sand. The
demonic erodes every sand castle. The ocean of being eventually
swallows every drop of life. But God is the perfect Father whose
unconditional love is eternally the way of life.

Jesus could say: "Moses said . . . but I say unto you." Why
could he speak so? Because he spoke not as a Pharisee, not as
a secondhand learner, not as a scribe, not even as a seminary
professor. The authority of Jesus was that of unconditional being
unto God. He was, lived, and taught firsthand. Such living and
teaching need no external defense. The basic rock of God's reality
cannot be safeguarded by arguments. The Sermon on the Mount
is the true catechism of the Christian church. Here life and
action, worship and work, being and witness come together.
Here join *kerygma* and *didache*. Here unite gospel and law. Here
creative freedom and depth wisdom flow from the unity of
life in God.

The Sermon on the Mount speaks to us today. *Be!* Be unto God!
Be unconditionally unto God! In God, be for all men. Thus you
will not break, but fulfill the law. Righteousness will be no burden,
but rather the creative freedom of love's going beyond duty,
unconditionally and inclusively. Do not strive to do, but make
the tree good and thus bear good fruit naturally. A life like this
needs no external protection. It is beyond anxiety because it
rests in God. It has found the state of blessedness even in
poverty and sorrow, even in persecution and rejection, for it
measures not its attainment in other terms than the being and

the doing of God's will. Rejoice, therefore, and be exceedingly glad, for the future is yours. In the deepest sense you shall inherit the earth. Creation was made for such as you; yes, even eternity is yours, for great is your reward in heaven.

Blessed be the God our Lord Jesus Christ who has given us such simple but real teachings to learn and to follow. Blessed be he who feeds us on the bread of life. Only because he is, and is all for us, can we live and love within the reality of the Sermon on the Mount. Therefore unto God be glory forever.

16.

The Reality of the Resurrection

> . . . because he preached Jesus and the resurrection. Acts 17:18.

As THE TITLE for his incisive inaugural address at the Harvard Divinity School, the late Dean Samuel Miller used the phrase, "To the Point Again." Employing a figure from Herman Melville, he took as his theme the thought that the pulpit should be the prow of the ship, not its poopdeck. In order to regain their lost intellectual leadership, Christian thinkers should dare once again to reexamine their faith to its very core.

In this long-remembered address, Dean Miller suggested that we have three basic choices in today's world of confused faith. First, we can cast our choice with the precritical believers who have zeal aplenty but, as the Bible puts it, not "according to knowledge." For the honest intellectual, he declared, such a choice is no longer open, for the burning fires of modernity ban all who have ever been exiled from the garden of naïve innocence from returning there.

The second possibility, he proposed, is the choice of those who resort to symbol or myth as props to shore up the sagging, even collapsing position of the Christian faith. These thinkers no longer believe that there is an objective counterpart to the supernatural world of precritical belief. They nevertheless use symbol and myth either to hide the fact of the utter collapse of the traditional faith or at best to preserve some vague values of the faith that is gone. These theologians have no God to worship and are left with thin and even empty myths and symbols with no power to save man from his own inner deterioration or his final self-destruction. Therefore Dean Miller advocated, as a third choice, that we return again to the rationalizing of our most elemental mysteries, especially whatever dependable knowledge we can glean from scientific inquiry.

Dean Miller's analysis, in my opinion, is generally sound. Religion should not be the hollow voice of the dead past, the wistful viewing of the churning past from the ship's stern. Even though so-called "modern man" is largely the artificial creation of a small clique of self-appointed intellectual elite, nevertheless, general education, as it becomes extended, makes it increasingly impossible either to continue in or to return to the precritical era of a naïve Christian faith.

Nor will those who depend on symbol and myth basically hold a significant following once people in general realize how gapingly impotent is the nearly empty vagueness to which the symbols and myths point. Only as long as there is strong faith in what is "more and other" than this world can symbols and myths speak with power to any generation.

We are left, therefore, with the third choice: we must return "to the point again"; we must make a new start. With this I agree, but not with Dean Miller's appeal to science as the base of religion. Science is important in its place; indeed, we must use it to the full with gratitude and diligence. But science describes what is, while religion prescribes what ought to be. More than that, faith prescribes not only what ought to be but what truly can be because of what ultimately is. Faith is primarily neither conditional nor imperative but indicative.

What, then, is the most effective way to return to the point again? I suggest simply to come to understand and to accept the reality of the Resurrection.

I

America's foremost theologian, Jonathan Edwards, once definitively declared, "The day of the Gospel most properly begins with

the resurrection of Christ." Before you conclude, however, that I
have betrayed my own analysis, which has just excluded the precritical position as a live option for today's honest and educated
man, let me explain what I mean by the Resurrection and then
let me illustrate how the reality of the Resurrection affects, transforms, and relevantly energizes the most critical issues of our
own day.

The Resurrection can be interpreted in several ways: (1)
the same Jesus, in the same body, rose from the grave literally
and made himself personally known to his disciples; (2) the
same Jesus, the personal spirit who had walked with his disciples,
in some way similar to his later appearance to Saint Paul on the
way to Damascus, communicated his presence to his disciples;
(3) God, the Eternal Spirit, convinced the disciples that this
Jesus whom they had known could not be held by death but
had rather conquered it; (4) God who is love revealed to the
disciples that the meaning of Jesus' life, as "the Son of his Love,"
alone is regnantly real and eternally victorious; (5) God already
in this life on earth said Yes to Jesus, to use Bultmann's famous
phrase, enabling him to rise above the anxiety and fear of
earthly death to the authentic freedom of a qualitative eternal
life which through him became accessible to all men.

The fanatical dogmatist, on the one hand, as the pseudo-
sophisticate on the other, will no doubt reject all positions but
his own. The open, searching thinker, however, will understand
that no position is without its own particular problems—his-
torical, philosophical, and theological—while all of them can
be used to stress what to me is the reality of the Resurrection.
The reality of the Resurrection is the transcendence of the personal over the subpersonal or antipersonal, of love over hate, of
spirit over the merely material, of life over death, of eternity
over time. Let us now apply this Resurrection reality, this Easter
truth, to the problems we face.

II

In personal life, if we begin here, Resurrection reality stands
for the victory of meaning over meaninglessness. If we will, we
can find the kind of life, the life of "the Man for others," as Bon-

hoeffer calls Jesus, that will attune us to the sources of meaning and afford us authentic satisfaction. Creative commitment to the reality of Ultimate Concern will lead to eternal life both here and now and forever. The truth of the Spirit of Concern opens up to the eternal Source of significance in which we can rest, and resting, work. If the reality of the Resurrection fails to minister to life itself at its center, it becomes empty. Life itself is an end, and should be accepted only as a means for the finding of more life. The life of concern itself engenders the kind of being that underlies all vital becoming and all needful doing.

Easter is the Event that declares life itself in its eternal dimension to be victorious over death. This truth of life, the reality of the Resurrection, can come only through the experience of the faith that grasps us where we live most deeply and transforms our life into personal victory—not away from the problems of the world, but within them and over them; not as escape from the threat of death, but as the life that overcomes death. Unless we are raised with Christ in this reality, Easter is no more than a mockery of man's best hopes.

Secondly, the reality of the Resurrection stands for the ultimate power in terms of which alone we can significantly change the world. A few years ago while I was living in Nashville, Tennessee, and teaching at Vanderbilt University, some of us were considered radical because we refused to accept segregation as normal and necessary and because we worked for and confidently lived the reality of human brotherhood among the races. Often I was chided for my quiet but persistent praying, witnessing, and working for a new day among people of all races.

Since then the nation has been moved by the persistent phrase, used even by President Johnson to Congress, "We shall overcome." The faith I had then and still have, however, was and is basically the power of Easter, the reality of the Resurrection. The power of God's love for human community is stronger potentially than all the combined forces of ignorance, inertia, and hatred. The regnant reality of the Resurrection underlies more than we know the total revolution that has seized our day.

The Resurrection reality, furthermore, is revolutionizing the church. No denomination, unless it is most backward or bigoted, dares to call itself alone "Christian." A few years ago, at the Chicago Sunday Evening Club, I ventured to suggest that the reality of the Resurrection could touch the feeling of self-sufficiency even on the part of the Roman Catholic church and make it want to open up to constructive new relations with Protestants. That sermon was published in 1962 in a book that did not then seem too much out-of-date. But by the time the British edition came out, I was embarrassed to be suggesting in it that the Roman Catholic church might become willing to rethink its age-old positions! Since the time of that writing, we have had Pope John and Vatican sessions that have staggered our imagination. Denominationalism as a final faith now looks like a dead end.

The church today is astir with self-criticism, courting a new day of service for the world on behalf of a better and fuller faith.

III

Beyond such ecumenical undertakings lies what the pope called "the wider ecumenism." Not only must we rethink the Christian faith; we must become open to all truths of all faiths, that with honesty and creative wrestling, we may find together the religion for one world. No divisive all-or-none religion will do, nor will any smooth or glib syncretism. But as people of one world, one humanity under God, we must work out what faith will most fully unite us all to seek a common will and to live a life of creative cooperation. The Resurrection has only limited reality unless its meaning and power can touch and make practicable for us this central problem of our times. Some of us in creative confrontation with world leaders of other faiths have already been working long enough at this task to know that we entertain no vain hope when we seek in depth to plumb the powers of reality that can generate the faith we need, both in line with the old religions and in creative transformation of them.

The celebration of Easter can have little meaning, furthermore, unless the reality of the Resurrection—the victory of life over death, of love over hate, of spirit over matter—can put our national loyalty into its proper place. At present we as a nation are threatening the very existence of human civilization because of our stubborn and bat-blind nationalism. We carry on wars thousands of miles away from American shores, prevent peoples from voting on their own governments, and generally support political reaction all in the name of national interest, and we cannot get out of our misguided involvements because of national pride. By our attempt to run the world we have undermined the United Nations and are courting ever new dangers.

Adlai Stevenson rightly said that since the whole world is a human family, war anywhere is civil war and any killing is fratricide. Along with the other nations we stand guilty. We must take a totally new course. University students are awakening to their responsibility and their stake in the future of the world. I believe that we can experience in this realm, too, the reality of the Resurrection—the victory of life over death, of love over hate and spirit over matter—to dissolve nationalism and build the organs and organizations for peace. We must radically revise or else go beyond the United Nations to include all nations constructively and healingly. The truth of Easter points us to this task.

But war and world destruction feed on the flames of supposedly "cold" war. War is a state of relations, a mood of mind before it is method. Organized and carefully promoted ill will precedes the shooting. Today those flames are the hot hatreds of capitalism versus communism. Both these names stand, more than we think, for stereotypes of the imagination. Both are to a large extent the myths of monstrous propaganda. All human systems are subject to change, and change they will, if given the right direction and motivation.

The world over, people want to live, want security, want order, want work, want meaning, want freedom as they understand the term, want to amount to something. They think and feel from within frameworks of civilization in which they are brought up and within which they are nourished. But immature man sharpens difference into stereotypes. Lust for power or

fear of the different creates oceans of ill will. We need today
to break down the whole apparatus of the cold war. We can do
so by the power of Easter. The reality of the Resurrection
maintains that things can be changed, that life can conquer
death, love overcome hate, and spirit win victory over matter.

We have never known, needless to say, more critical times,
but neither have we known days of fuller opportunity. History
is flexible to change. Jesus was everlastingly right in suggesting
that it will be done to us according to our faith. Our need now
is the kind of faith that will generate vision with motivation,
the seeing of the goal along with the will to reach it. We can
spend millions in motivation research and still perish, for men
are moved only by the truth in which they genuinely believe.
They will countenance no easy or false answers.

All our problems of race and religion, of hot wars and cold
wars, will fail of solution apart from the right faith to give
men hope. All plans and schemes for national or international
betterment will come to naught apart from the determined will
to win that is rooted in the nature of ultimates. We can change
laws through demonstrations and we can revise the history of
power through organization of people, through strikes and boy-
cotts, through rent strikes and political connivance. We must
not underestimate the power of radical action to secure new
rights for men in many areas of life. The people are throwing
off their yokes of yesterday and marching, marching to a new
day of freedom.

Unfortunately, however, as in my native Sweden, one can
institute social and political solutions for the envy of all the
world, and one can spread general education broadcast in the
land without learning to live meaningfully and with zest, however great these achievements be in themselves. Life depends
on meaning, the meaning that motivates, the reality that gives
life zest, the truth that calls for adventure of mind and spirit.
While acknowledging all the good that can come through power
politics, I know that this method and this mood will fall short
of the goal of human community in depth of attainment and in
height of hope.

The final power is the reality of the Resurrection, the appeal finally to the Source of significance and to the Ultimate Power of personal purpose. We need the reestablishment of morality without moralism, of righteousness without legalism, of faith in God without fanaticism. We can have new lives and a new world at the price only of a new-found faith in the reality of the Resurrection. God always "buries his undertakers," and genuine faith in his love for all men engenders the creative concern that can work the miracles of hope. All education is for learning to live together as men, to learn the truth of Easter that life finally is more real than death, love more powerful than hate, and spirit more lasting than all men's material achievements.

17.

Three Gifts of the Spirit

> *When the Spirit of truth comes, he will guide you into all the truth.* John 16:13.
> *Hope does not disappoint us, because God's love has been poured into our hearts through the Holy Spirit.* Romans 5:5.
> *The fruit of light is found in all that is good and right and true.* Ephesians 5:9.

I BELIEVE THAT Pentecost was an historic occurrence, but I believe also that Pentecost should be every day. I want to talk about the Pentecostal experience of the Spirit, because I believe it is the most neglected and misunderstood experience in the Christian church. "The Holy Spirit" has become a pious phrase, rather than a vivid and solid and serious reality.

I have, to be sure, a personal reason for speaking and writing on the Holy Spirit: I was born on Pentecost. The first time my mother held me in her arms she said, "This child is born on the day of Pentecost, the day of the Spirit. I dedicate him to the ministry of the Spirit." Although I never knew of this until many years later, somehow I could not go into anything except the ministry. I tried. I was offered several tempting positions to teach secular subjects in universities. But I was never happy in the prospect. I had been dedicated to the Spirit and could not escape that fact.

On this topic of the Holy Spirit, then, I want to deal with three gifts of the Spirit. Traditionally there are seven, but three are enough for one time!

150

I

The first gift of the Spirit is that of *the open mind*. "When the Spirit of truth comes, he will guide you into *all* the truth." Augustine said that the lover of truth need fear no man's censure. Either he is right and then he cannot change, or he is wrong and then he wants to change. Therefore whoever is really open to the truth need have no fear of being corrected.

Calvin said that whoever does not accept truth, from whatever quarter it comes, insults the Holy Spirit because the Holy Spirit in the Bible is defined as the Spirit of truth. It is a matter of abiding in Christ, not just in such a narrow way that we land in a narrow Christocentric truth, but believing also that the Holy Spirit "will guide you into all the truth."

In our day it is difficult for people to identify themselves with a concrete religion. Ever since Kant, we have heard that it is impossible to be loyal to a concrete religion and yet be completely open to all truth. In our day Karl Jaspers, a profound philosopher, is saying the same thing. In *Philosophical Faith and Revelation,*° a great book, he says that we have to choose between commitment to a concrete religion, in which case we close our mind to universal truth, or accepting a philosophic stance in which we are willing to listen to truth no matter what. My conviction is that those who genuinely accept the Christian faith at its deepest know that they have to be open minded. They have to receive the gift of *the open mind* because the Holy Spirit shall lead us into all the truth.

Of course there are two types of truth. There is the truth of merely descriptive phenomena. That is one kind of truth. But there is a deeper truth. The deeper truth is that of personal relationships. I can analyze the desk before me by means of chemistry, because it is an object open to my search. But I cannot analyze a single one of you. I cannot put a fluoroscope in you and see what you think and feel, unless you reveal yourself to me. This is the deepest and most profound truth of personal relations. The truth of right personal relations is

° Tr. E. B. Ashton (New York: Harper & Row, 1967).

the truth of concern. I believe all truth is subservient to and ancillary to this fundamental truth of concern.

In one sense the truth that we have in concern and the truth that is of concern are the same, because God is truth. God is Ultimate Concern, and when we live in this concern for the truth we live in God, because God as the Holy Spirit is defined as truth. Therefore no one can genuinely be open to integrity and concern, the two main pillars, the twin pillars of the Christian faith in Christ, and not covet with all his heart an open-minded, open-ended attitude. "When the Spirit of truth comes, he will guide you into all the truth."

II

The second gift of the Holy Spirit is the gift of *the warm heart*, the love of God which "the Holy Spirit shall pour into your heart."

In the Christian faith, when it is rightly understood, there is no distinction that separates the open mind and the warm heart. They are together in the Bible itself. God is love and he that loves not cannot know God, for God is love (1 John 4:7–8). Love and knowledge go together within the very Christian faith.

Some people do not realize that unless we understand with our total self, with our total involvement, with our total personality, we cannot understand the full truth. Therefore they narrow truth down to a little academic method and construct for themselves an artificial metaphysics and escape the depth and reality of the effective life. Some people are really afraid of feelings, but those who understand reality are not. They *are* afraid of the improper use of feeling, of the feelings that do not stand up to the critical and careful mind. On the contrary, we need to remember always that the fundamental need of every human being is for God. And God is love.

Clemens Benda in his book, *The Image of Love,* * says that every human being at the depth of his life longs for love. He

---

* New York: Free Press, 1961.

needs love. But most people dry up and shrivel up because they are afraid of love. They have seen so much false love that they do not trust it, says Benda, or they have never seen enough genuine love, and therefore they run away from it. But as Ashley Montagu rightly says in *The Humanization of Man*,‡ anyone who wants to study the history of anthropology and particularly the rearing of children will find that children can be brought up with every physical and social advantage and still fail to mature, fail to find the fullness of life as much as less "advantaged" children who are confronted with or endowed with genuine love. He gives an illustration of a nursery where despite the best of scientific care practically all the children were dying. The doctors did not know why. Eventually they employed an old woman who had an almost pathological need to love. When a case seemed hopeless they gave the child to this woman who would love it into life.

The late Professor Maslow of Brandeis University used to say that people need love as much as they need salt. Yes, we need the warm heart, the affective heart. In religion we cannot short-circuit this need. When I was doing my doctoral studies at Harvard and serving a church besides, I had to work from four-thirty in the morning until eleven at night. I came home one day and found that we had callers. One of the guests asked my three-year-old son Frederick what he was going to be when he grew up. To my amazement Frederick replied, "I am not going to Harvard and dry up."

I doubt that the insight was his own, but there was a lot of truth to it. In our academic life, in our great search for truth, we often underestimate the part that the depth and reality of our feelings play. Therefore, it is important that the Holy Spirit gives us not only an open mind but also a warm heart. The Holy Spirit is going to pour love into your heart. That is the promise.

We suffer from the stanch of affection that comes from self-promotion and the stoppage of warmth that comes from self-protection. Only our living in Reality, in the Spirit, can open

‡ New York: Grove Press, 1964.

our lives to the springs of affection that enliven and enrich life.
The Bible says the Holy Spirit shall *pour* love into our hearts.
He can give us *the warm heart.*

III

The third gift of the Spirit that I want to offer is that of
the effective hand. No phrase quite expresses what I want to
say. Surely "the helpful hand" falls short of my meaning. What
I am really after is the appropriate act, "the fruit of light"
that "is found in all that is good and right and true." There is
no substitute in our day for appropriate action. It is a wonderful
thing that the Christian church is awakening to the need to
take a stand in all areas of life.

Action is now in our blood. This is now the vogue, at least
among theologians. One of my theological friends, given to
"demonstrating," was asked, "Have you been in prison?" One
who all his life has suffered for a cause, replied mildly, "No,
not since it became popular."

All of us, these days, are concerned about living out the
Christian message in race, living out the Christian message
among the denominations, living it out for world peace. All of
us are concerned about doing something to end the war in
Vietnam and getting China into the United Nations. All of us
are trying in our own way and according to our own understanding, to do whatever can be done for peace. We may have
different methods and different approaches, but all of us are
working toward this end. And it is needful.

Perhaps I had better say one word of caution. Some people
now are preaching a social gospel that is not according to the
Holy Spirit. They are telling us that when we join a protest
march or a picket line, worship becomes optional, for the living
God is no longer necessary. But this is a denial of our text.
It is the Holy Spirit who shall lead us in the appropriate attitude
into the appropriate act.

We want to pass from an era of mere personal goodness into
that of social righteousness. Let us not underestimate personal
goodness. The Bible is right when it says, "make the tree good"

(Matt. 12:33). My evangelical friends are right that unless we make *people* good we shall never make the *world* good merely by external opportunities. The fundamental road to a new day lies always through the renewed personality, the reoriented personality, the reconstituted personality. All of us therefore need first of all personal goodness. But personal goodness must eventuate, must issue into, a relationship of social concern and social righteousness. When personal goodness and social righteousness have been won, then finally, truth will be ours.

Jesus stood among them and said, "Receive ye the Holy Spirit. If you are my disciples you must receive the Holy Spirit."

The Holy Spirit is no pious phrase, no glib expression. The Holy Spirit is opening our lives in integrity to the open mind, being ready for all truth. The Holy Spirit is the warmth of heart that dares to live intimately with the family, that dares to live closely with colleagues, that dares to live widely with all people, accepting them because we have ourselves become genuine selves. The Holy Spirit is the One who leads us not only to personal goodness but into social righteousness and truth. His gift is therefore the effective hand as well as the mind that is alert and the heart that throbs for our fellow-man.

18.

The Perfect Prescription
for Church Renewal

*The grace of the Lord Jesus Christ and the love of
God and the fellowship of the Holy Spirit be with
you all.* 2 Corinthians 13:14.

ONE DAY I WAS JARRED twice. First, a visiting British pacifist had
called me "cynical" because I did not agree with his hopeful
opinion that the institutional church in its totality might initiate
and unilaterally sponsor total disarmament and world peace.
This well-known pacifist said that all we have to do is to *tell*
the churches, and we will get peace. I was not so optimistic.

Secondly, I was jarred during my seminar that day, in which
the students were discussing the nature of the church. One of
them started by saying that the best way to renew the church
is to kill it. He said, "Let us abolish the church and the church
will not have any problems." The next person suggested, "If
you start small prayer groups, that will take care of all our
problems." A third student proposed "covenant groups." "These
covenant groups will change the whole church," he promised.
As I sat there listening, I was sad. I felt that the analysis was
too shallow, too superficial to strike the depth problems of the
church. As I listened I wondered what the perfect prescription
for church renewal would be.

156

I

I have come to believe that the perfect prescription is voiced in the benediction: "The grace of the Lord Jesus Christ and the love of God and the fellowship of the Holy Spirit be with you all."

I first came to this understanding in the middle of the night. I was praying about the church's state, grieved that I could not find more depth and power to minister to the problem. As I was praying I was struck by this thought: the benediction! Why don't we utilize the benediction as the prescription for the renewal of the church?

But my remembrance of the benediction that night was mistaken. I began working out the prescription this way: "The love of God the Father, the grace of our Lord Jesus Christ, and the fellowship of the Holy Spirit." In the morning when I looked at 2 Corinthians I saw that it did not say that. I looked in several other translations and they did not say it that way either. Since then I have observed that many ministers similarly switch the order in the benediction, putting "The love of God the Father," before "the grace of our Lord Jesus Christ." It is not biblical, but it is logical. It is the order in which we think of the Trinity. We start with God, then the incarnation, then the fellowship. But that is not the way it is written.

I began to wonder then why the benediction was given this way. Why does it not start the way I would start it? I began to understand that there are many reasons. One is that we men in history are sinners and need to begin with grace, rather than with love. "Love" is a general term that refers to the nature and purpose of God in his relationship to men. But grace is love in action against the background of our sin and our concrete problems. Therefore, instead of understanding God merely theoretically or speculatively, we need to understand God actually in the situation in which we find ourselves.

The great revolution in the life of the famous British preacher, Peter Taylor Forsyth, came in these terms. He said, in effect, "My fundamental revolution came when I was turned from a lover of love to an object of grace. For years I loved to preach about the love of God. It was wonderful. But nothing really hap-

pened in terms of power, until I became an object of grace. I
had to stop being merely a lover of love, a theoretical pro-
claimer of something, and become an object of grace."

In the second place, we know God in history; we know God
as incarnate love. As the expression goes, we say "God" but
think "Jesus." The model of God's love, this concrete love, we
find in human history in Jesus. Kierkegaard long ago in his
Philosophical Fragments distinguished between two kinds of
universal or general truth. One kind he called a "Socratic occasion." A Socratic occasion is a truth so general that the more
the messenger or the bringer of it disappears, the better it is
for the truth, the more clear it is. The other kind, which he
termed a "Christian moment," is also a universal truth, but one
where the messenger is so completely, intimately and intrinsically bound up with the coming of that truth, that you cannot
do away with the messenger without doing away with the message. *The messenger is himself the message.* In Christ we do not
see a speculative, abstract truth alone. We see truth embodied,
we see truth made flesh, we see truth made one of us. Therefore
we have to begin with "the grace of the Lord Jesus Christ," a
truth that can be generalized but never abstracted from, taken
away from, or divorced from its relation to persons.

Furthermore, the grace of the Lord Jesus Christ is this concrete grace that he has given us because he himself has experienced it. This is something that most Christians fail to
understand. They fail to understand that the Holy Trinity has a
funnel or a focus through the Son and through the Spirit into the
world, into the very Christian community. As the three Cappadocians * maintained, the Spirit proceeds from God the
Father through the Son into the world and into our very concrete and real humanity. Saint Augustine, in a famous passage,
says that we must be saved by the same grace by which that
man Jesus Christ was saved. To some people this sounds strange
because we have forgotten the humanity of Jesus. We have let
ourselves become docetic and have sacrificed any real doctrine

* The three Cappadocians were Gregory of Nazianzus, Basil of Caesarea,
and Gregory of Nyssa who lived in the fourth century and who interpreted
the Nicene creed so that it was accepted by the Eastern bishops.

of the humanity of Jesus, without which we can have no real incarnation.

Jesus himself experienced our temptations, he experienced the human self-drive, he had to cry, "Not my will but thy will!" Jesus himself knew these our weaknesses and failings, but in his union, in his identification, in his incarnation of God's spirit, of God's very presence in him, he found the conquering of temptation, the overcoming of sin, and the opening to the full resources of the grace of God in human history whereby he, as one of us, could become the one through whom we can go to the Father. Or, as Irenaeus and later church fathers said, "God became human to make us divine." We often forget that there is one in human history who so participated in the life of God, and so participated in the life of man, that we can say, "the grace of the Lord Jesus Christ," knowing that his grace is not merely external, but from one who understands. Because he has participated in our situation, we can share in his grace.

II

Next, "the love of God." Even though we have seen love in history, as the grace of Christ, we need to know and comfort our hearts by the faith that the Creator is Love, the ultimate Compassion, the Ultimate Concern. Think with Browning, that "the All-Great" is "the All-Loving too." * Think of the vastness of the galaxies which overwhelm modern man so that he has learned to know the immensities of the universe, and yet his attempts to feel himself into it are impossible. Browning goes on to say, "a heart beats here." A heart beats not only in the soul, a heart beats also in the universe, behind the universe, and through the universe.

One of our fundamental problems in modern Christian theology is that some of our theologians have so whittled away God's work in creation that we know God as the Ultimate Concern, as the power for authentic being, but this knowledge is merely in

* An Epistle Containing the Strange Medical Experience of Karshish, the Arab Physician, line 305.

our own faith. We do not see him in relation to the whole world
and to providence. Without this relation we have no ultimate
hope, no ultimate faith that God is in charge and that we can
trust him completely.

The ultimate faithfulness for the future is also involved here.
Can you trust God not only in the Christ of history but in the
all of history, and for all of history? Many people read the newspaper and *Time* magazine and then they go to church and find
that the two worlds don't really belong together. Sometimes I
worship the best when I take those awful morning newspapers,
open them up, look at them, hold them up in the light of the
infinite Concern. I almost see the eyes of God, the tragic,
weary eyes of God, in relation to my poor little concerns. I lift up
the world's problems and I say, "The world need not be this way,
if we as Christians dare to accept the grace that is ours, the love
of God." When we read the newspaper—the dreadful statistics
of war, crime, poverty, racial injustice, moral degradation—
when we are aware of all these things, the love of God ought
to show so deeply within and through our lives that history begins to change.

The Communists believe that history can be changed. They
are sure of it. That history can be changed is the very order of
science, the very order of interpreting dialectic materialism.
Change has to happen. What has happened to us Christians?
We should not be satisfied simply with going to church on Sunday, but we should believe in the depth of our hearts in such
a way that history becomes concretely and ultimately changed.
God is in charge. "The love of God . . . be with you all."

One of the deepest wrestlings I have ever had with a subject
was in connection with an invitation from the London Missionary
Society to write on the problem of atonement and the missionary
relation to the brutality of human history. This is the modern
Christian's fundamental problem. How can we believe that atonement does not merely apply to some personal faith, to some personal forgiveness, but that atonement applies to all of human
history as well as all of nature? The God who cares ultimately
for each individual is the same One who has created all. His im-
mensity is also intimacy; God cares for all and each.

In a church I served years ago, one of the deacons was a manufacturer. It was in the days of the depression and he was losing his business. He was an honest man, faithful to his church. One day I felt called upon to preach on the text, "God knows." As I preached I saw this tired, weary, defeated man almost literally straighten up moment by moment. After the service he took my hand and said, "Nels, you helped me this morning. I can stand anything if God really knows and cares." And he went out to face his difficult problems. Even the great skeptic Nietzsche said, "Man can stand any how if he knows the why." Huston Smith's book, *Condemned to Meaning,* ° is an interesting treatment of this subject of why and how.

A denominational leader of Japanese parentage told how as a boy he and his parents were taken out of their California home and put into a concentration camp, even though they had done no wrong at all. They were good Americans. American born, he felt himself an American, and his mother, the proud daughter of a Samurai family, died out of humiliation. He spoke of his life behind barbed wire. He said, "I just felt hate. I wanted to hate all Americans for what they were doing. But I was a Christian and I began to concentrate on the love of God. I said, 'Can I still believe in the love of God?' Finally I decided, 'Yes, in spite of what is being done to us, even though we are innocent, I can believe in the love of God.'"

Through his understanding and acceptance of the love of God he found it possible to forgive us. He found it possible not to become bitter. He found it possible to go out and become constructive as an American once again. The love of God is no abstract, faraway understanding. It is in creation, it is in history. But it comes right down concretely to your life and to my life in every personal relationship.

III

"The grace of the Lord Jesus Christ and the love of God and the fellowship of the Holy Spirit be with you all." This is the

° New York: Harper & Row, 1964.

perfect prescription for the renewal of the church. The fellowship of the true church—I am not talking about the institutional
church with all its problems and failings—is the fellowship of
the Spirit because the church is constituted by the Spirit; the
soul of the church is the Spirit. In our true nature we *are* first
of all *spirit* and only secondarily *have being*. We become ourselves only by becoming what we most deeply are. We are of
God, we are of this corporate reality. Beneath the feverish in-
dividuations of selves, we become real, become what we truly
are, wrapped up in the bundle of God's purpose for us, as *one*
ultimately in the love which is in Christ Jesus.

Mary Baker Eddy says that we are God's idea and as God's
idea we are perfect. All we have to do is to realize what we are
and then our problems are solved. I appreciate Mary Baker
Eddy's interpretation, but it is not quite enough. It is true that
we can become only what we most fundamentally or potentially
are. We can become nothing else. But *becoming is real*. God's
pedagogy is real. God has created us for a purpose. He has made
us to go our own way in ignorance and struggling and suffering,
in order that we might be won to light, to love, and to ourselves
in our true community. Therefore it is true that when we really
accept the fellowship of the Holy Spirit, we accept ourselves. We
accept ourselves not as we are, but as we are destined to become;
and the way we are destined to become is the deepest thing
we are. Only by becoming can being become what it is!

Hinduism says that life is fragmentary, life is a matter of
ignorance, life is a matter of unsatisfactory knowledge and experience. Therefore we must believe in the essential self that
always is. Mary Baker Eddy is right there. Buddhism says, "No,
we have a suffering, illusory experience. Therefore we must
understand that no experience is real, and neither is the chain
that binds them together real. Fundamentally there is no self."
But the Christian faith says, "No. We *are in becoming*. We are
basically potential selves, so that what we are potentially is
what we most properly are." What we most actually are is not
the end, is not the truth. God has made us for himself and we
are restless until we abide in him. Therefore, when we extend
this fellowship of the Spirit, we extend to each and to all what he

and what all most properly are. Therefore, our total selves is our hope. A child can only become what it truly is: a child destined to grow. We are God's children called to become God's mature sons.

The ecumenical movement can be genuinely ecumenical only when it is one in the true church, one in the true spirit, one in the true reality. The wider ecumenism can be nothing in terms of one spirit here and one spirit there. The wider ecumenism that Pope Paul has talked about must fundamentally be the understanding of the Light that lights everyone that comes into the world. Because we are all made by this Light and for this Light, we can all come to this Light. Therefore we have the fellowship in the Spirit. Therefore our total self as persons and as individuals, together and as distinct, must be fulfilled by the one Spirit or the one Love which is Christ and is all. There is no other hope as persons for you and for me. There is no other hope for community and there is no other hope for any aspect of human experience than the fulfillment of our deepest and total self in the reality of who God is. That and that alone is the reality of unimunity, God's fuller goal for each and all.

In the spirit of the wider ecumenism I will quote Lao Tse, the Chinese writer and prophet. He says: "To have been cast in this human form is to us already a source of joy. How much greater joy beyond our conception it is to know that that which is now in human form may undergo countless transitions with only the infinite to look forward to."

I believe this very profoundly. I believe that when we die we are not going to be frozen stiff into some permanent form of being. I believe that when we die God has eternity in store for us in terms of growth, in terms of education, in terms of what ear has not heard nor eye seen. If there is any human being who believes with all his heart out of all his study and his decisions that this life is not all, it is I. I have thought this through in every direction and prayed it through in every direction.

All I know is that life after death will not be the continuation of this life just as it is, nor will it be the cessation of it. Paul Tillich said this in his Harvard lectures, using almost these words. Life will be something that goes beyond our understand-

ing in terms of some transformation, that continues what is best
and highest but goes beyond it so far that we cannot even
imagine, let alone understand.

When the fellowship of the Holy Spirit really begins to take
this little individual self of ours and unite it in terms of a deeper
and truer being, and to set us free for further growth and development, then there shall be something that we cannot understand in terms of the depth and reality which God has prepared
for us.

The church needs renewal, more than we can say. Only a new
grasp of faith can work the miracle that is now needed. Only a
strong measure of reality can heal the broken and helpless community seeking to become real again. To renew the church
we must go beyond "church renewal" by the fulfilling formula.
The perfect prescription for the renewal and fulfillment of the
church is our acceptance in faith and life of this all-embracing
benediction: "The grace of the Lord Jesus Christ and the love
of God and the fellowship of the Holy Spirit be with you all."

19.

All That Matters

> In Christ Jesus neither circumcision nor uncircumcision is of any avail, but faith working through love. Galatians 5:6.

"THE ONLY THING that counts," says our text according to *The New English Bible*, "is faith active in love." Even more forceful is Monsignor Knox's translation: "The faith that finds its expression in love is all that matters." *

All of us are quite naturally suspicious of superlatives. We question all extremes, certainly all total statements. But our text gives us an extreme statement, a total statement to end all statements. All that matters is faith working through love.

Can we really state in one formula "all that matters," "the only thing that counts," the total response to all we value, to all we need, to all we crave? Naturally, we have to presuppose our own concrete experience. No formula can ever be a substitute for life. No blueprint will ever take the place of a bridge that has to be built. Just try to cross the Hudson on a blueprint!

No formula can take the place of life, or can give us that total variegated spectrum of actual living. But a formula can give us a context for life, a pattern, a perspective for understanding and

---

* *The New English Bible* (New York: Oxford University Press, Cambridge University Press, 1970). *The Holy Bible,* tr. Ronald Knox (New York: Sheed & Ward, Inc., 1954).

organizing our lives; something that can direct our lives, the world that we are, and the world that we meet. The Apostle Paul has given precisely such a formula—a pattern, a perspective that is all-embracing, all-discriminating, all-intensive, and all-directive. "Faith that finds its expression in love is all that matters."

I

This pattern is important to the Christian faith because it gives the possibility of creative self-expression. You cannot imitate a personality without becoming stultified. You cannot imitate a principle without becoming inflexible. But you can use a pattern because a pattern is precisely for the creative adaptation to need. A woman buys a dress pattern sized according to a perfect model, perhaps one known to a previous generation as a "perfect thirty-six." Then she takes this pattern and somehow or other adapts it to her own needs, a little bulge here or a little lack there. Most of us simply cannot fit the model; the pattern has to be altered to fit our figure. The same is true for a man buying a suit.

One of my daughters seemed to have a hard time buying dresses, and I thought that was ridiculous because she is such a beautiful girl. But she said, "Daddy, you should come along with me and see!" "I will," I said. "We'll go downtown and pick up a dress or two." We went to Jordan Marsh, to Filene's—all over Boston. We worked for hours and nothing fit. Zippers bulged, waistlines wrinkled. Finally, over the saleswoman's protests, my daughter went to some subteen racks and found something short-waisted enough to fit her. It was not as easy as I had thought. So it is in life. It is not as easy as it seems to take this perfect model of the love of God in Christ and apply it particularly and concretely to our individual bulges or lacks.

Faith that finds its expression in love is all that matters. We all live by faith, for we *are* our faith. Our faith is our total living, our whole response in and to life. By what we are, we show our faith. By what we do, we show our faith. By what we think, will, and feel, we show our faith. By what we expect, we reveal our faith. Faith necessarily centers in ultimates. Faith centers in what to us is most important and most real. To live is to decide. No one can escape decision as to the total meaning of life.

It is one of the greatest mysteries of all life that no matter how close you get to someone else, that person cannot share your most intimate understanding and meaning, nor feel your feelings in such a way that you do not have to live your own life, make your own decisions. The choice may be weak, confused, ignorant. But even to continue living is a stance, a posture, a judgment of faith.

We all live by faith. No one can prove God. This is obvious, because God is the ultimate presupposition of all reality, of all values, of all experience. No one can prove a presupposition, because if you prove it, it is no longer a presupposition. Thus it is perfectly obvious that all of us have to live by faith. The true faith centers in the living God, in the Faithful One. The great German philosopher, Heidegger, said in his old age that the fundamental meaning of knowledge is that being reveals itself. But those of us who have come to know God know that the fundamental nature of knowledge is not merely that being reveals itself, but that God reveals himself. The personal Spirit in whom we participate reveals himself.

Faith is much more our being grasped than our grasping. It is far more being possessed than possessing. The faith that we have to hang on to is no real faith at all. The only faith that matters is the faith that we cannot get away from. It is either the faith that we have to have when everything goes dead wrong, and then we have to make our decision, or else the faith that when we are relaxed and happy makes us just naturally think about and do the thing that is most real to us. That is the kind of faith that is our faith—not what we say we believe, but what actually informs and directs our decisions. Full or true faith is a state of being possessed or grasped and lightened and directed by the living God. The only faith that counts, "all that matters," is the faith that finds its expression in love. We have to live by faith. This is a fascinating thing, because love and faith come close together.

An outstanding Harvard professor came to Andover Newton,

where I was teaching at the time, to speak to our students about faith. "God is the faithful one," he said. "The fundamental thing about Christian faith is that God is the faithful one on whom we can count." Afterward he came home with me for a meal, and very abjectly, almost sheepishly, he began to apologize.

"What are you apologizing for?" I asked.

"I didn't mean to hurt you," he replied. "I came and spoke about faith as ultimate, but I know that you believe that love is ultimate. I did not mean to throw a thunderbolt. Please forgive me." I said, "My dear friend, you have advocated everything that I stand for, and I accept you warmly and happily."

II

My deepest and fullest definition of love is precisely that *God is faithful*. We can depend upon him, even when we cannot see what he is doing, even when we cannot understand all his ways. God is faithful. Therefore there is no dichotomy between love on the one hand and faith on the other. God cares, God cares for all, and God's care will prevail. This is the fundamental meaning when we say that we have seen the sovereign love of God in Christ.

Some of you have read the well-known books by my sister, Thyra Ferré Bjorn, about our mother and other members of the family.* Mother was a saint of God. My sister is an exceptional person and writer, but not even she could portray the depth of devotion and confident faith of my mother. Once when I had not seen Mother for some time, I made a trip to her home in Florida. I was very happy as I approached the house. Of course she was waiting for me. Before I could get to the house with my bags, she ran out on the lawn, and I expected her to say how glad she was to see me. But no.

"Nels," she said, her first greeting after this long absence, "can I think anything too good about God?"

Surprised, I said, "No, Mother, of course you can't."

* *Papa's Wife* (1955); *Papa's Daughter* (1958); *Mama's Way* (1959); *Dear Papa* (1963); *Once Upon a Christmas* (1964); *Home Has a Heart* (1968). All published by Holt, Rinehart and Winston.

"Then," she said, "nothing else matters."

That is exactly our text. All that matters is faith that finds its expression in love. Mother was ailing, she was old, life was hard, but if she could trust God, then nothing else mattered. Faith that finds its expression in love is all that matters.

Karl Barth was able to show that God is a transcendent reality, the ultimate One who rules. But Barth shows that God rules for the sake of man because He is love. Is there a difference here? No, it is the same thing. Emil Brunner says that faith presupposes love. You cannot believe in someone unless he is well disposed toward you, unless he can do what he has promised. Therefore faith presupposes love. Bultmann, in his emphasis on finding faith as the freedom for the future, is only saying that we need not be anxious in our seeking for authentic existence, because fundamentally, if we have faith, we have that reality or we are grasped by that reality which can make for authentic existence.

The Bible is wonderful. One of the last things that I did for my son when he left home was to choose a Bible verse for him as he requested. I chose the verse, "God is able to make all grace abound toward you; that ye, always having all sufficiency in all things, may abound to every good work" (2 Cor. 9:8, KJV). That is what faith is. Faith is the assurance, as someone has said, that the measure of the practicable, the measure of what can be done, is not our past experience but is God's call, God's promises. Therefore we can expect great things from God because of the nature of faith.

Faith in God, then, is best expressed by the Cross and the Resurrection. The Cross and the Resurrection are God's deeds, his eternal promises that his love goes all the way, no matter what. He can do what he has promised and therefore beyond death is life eternal, beyond death is resurrection, beyond love's failures are love's victories. We often hear that God is unconditional. But he is not unconditional, if by that we mean that he has unconditional being. Of course not. Then he could not relate himself. God is not unconditional being, but unconditional love. God is unconditional love, and therefore I agree with Charles Hartshorne when he says we had better change our language and say that God is all-conditional. God loves in all conditions. He loves "no matter what." Therefore we can trust our anxious hearts. We can trust God's care for us, so that we should accept whatever comes, be it sunny days or rainy days, not in the spirit merely of resignation but in the spirit of faith. God can use any and all conditions, and use us in any and all conditions, to his glory and to human helpfulness.

III

Such faith in God as love calls for a new trust in God, a new way of working that will be meaningful and that will generate the right kind of motivation. I been trying to dedicate the depth of my life toward finding and writing about those resources of truth that are consistent with these biblical promises. We have never taken the Christian faith—God as spirit, God as love, the personal Spirit, Love—and worked these out as the categories, as the framework of thought in terms of which we must formulate the Christian faith. We have always borrowed from Plato, we have borrowed from Aristotle, we have borrowed from Hegel, we have borrowed from Kant, we have borrowed even from the philosophers of linguistic analysis and existentialism, and then we say, "Look! How many problems we have with the Christian faith!"

When I examine the "problems" I see that the problems are inherent in the philosophy we have borrowed, and not in the faith. The time has come for us, not to say that we are not going to use any language, any thought forms, but resolutely to wrestle with these thought forms and with the problems pertaining to the ultimate, until we can in honesty and competence speak in all areas of life. That is my mission. Pray that such a faith find its expression in love in theology, pray that it find its expression in motivation for a new kind of living that we have re-formed.

Some people are afraid of the word *reform*. Reform, to some people, means radicalism. To others it connotes the stuffiness of something that is past. But all reform means is to find a form again, to re-form. We recover a form or we find a form that is consistent with the best kind of understanding, the best kind of direction. We need a reformation in our day. The reformation we need is neither an irresponsible radicalism nor a stuffy conservatism, but a reformation that is so centered in human need and in God's purpose for the world, that we shall in honesty be able to live and to think out this faith about which we talk. The time has come for us to go beyond justice into that kind of ultimate concern for all men that shall release us into a free and full motivation. Not only shall it release us because we have a meaning and a motivation, but also because we find a method of living and an ultimate understanding that shall be consistent with it.

A society where love finds full expression is the universal society with maximum acceptance of all and openness to all. It is a society with active, intelligent concern for maximum freedom and opportunity for each individual and each group to find and to develop this way of living as our best selves, and our talents as persons, with creative distinctiveness, no matter what our particular situation or task in life. Such faith will find its maximum maturity in love.

But we should not always be seeking.

I never tire of confessing how very much I love gardening. But I find myself so often watching for bugs and spraying and picking off the dead blossoms that I never really enjoy the garden. Then I say, "The flowers are beautiful. Thank God for them. I'll spray and I'll pick off the dead blooms, but fundamentally I am going to enjoy the garden." The hummingbird flutters its wings nervously until all of a sudden it centers in and finds the nectar. Then there is stillness in motion, while it feeds and enjoys. If we discuss religion too much or are too anxious about our faith, we have not found faith.

The feeding hummingbird is no longer nervous. Its relationship to the nectar is not static. It is a dynamic relationship, but it is focused and resting and finding. So we are not going to stop our activity. We are not going to stop our working. But we are going to find something that is so real—faith's nectar—

that even in our working we rest and even in our resting we work, until we find that all that matters is faith that finds its expression in love.

We need to find the faith that matters, that gives meaning, motivation, maturity, and love. Then a vital, valiant faith will produce all needed work. To find life's core is to find the faith that will always matter because it finds its expression in love.

20.
Eternity and Now

Known unto God are all his works from the beginning of the world. Acts 15:18 (KJV).

THERE IS ALWAYS fascination in the problem of foreknowledge and freedom. How can God be completely in charge of the world if he does not know what is going to happen? On the other hand, how can man be genuinely free, and how can his freedom make a real difference if God from all eternity knows what he is going to do?

Paul's preaching to the Gentiles was justified by James before the Council of Jerusalem by the assertion that God knew from all eternity what he was going to do at that council. God knew that Paul was going to proclaim the message of salvation to the Gentiles. God knew that Paul was going to break through the Jewish system of segregation. He knew that Paul was going to break down barriers and make the Christian faith universal. Indeed, God had approved this from all eternity.

People are always fascinated by fatalism, by the idea of inevitable destiny. What proportion of the world's population has believed in astrology? Some still do. I found, to my surprise, as I visited and talked intimately with some of the Christian leaders of Asia, that when you scratch even a Christian deep down you find that some of them still believe more strongly than they like to admit in astrology.

Not only Islam, but the Protestant Reformers believed in God's complete foreknowledge. Not only Calvin and Luther, but even more strongly Zwingli accepted predestination of some kind. Today the Marxists believe in the inevitability of history. They believe that somehow or other by changing the control of the means of production, eventually all classes but the working class will disappear. Thus they will overthrow democracy and establish a good life for all people as the state itself withers away.

Notice the paradox. The Christians, the non-Christians, and the Marxists all feel the same way—things must happen. All right. Therefore we must work the harder. This is not logical, is it? Things must happen; therefore we must work the harder! We should think that psychology would work the other way— things must happen, therefore why should we do anything about it?

Perhaps this is the reason: there is also, on the other hand, a continual call for freedom. Somehow, at the depth of man's being, at the very depth of his spirit, there is a constant cry that his life must make a difference. What he is doing is not just something that has to be done mechanically, but something that matters, something that is important because he is doing it. Many theologians are positive that if freedom is not real, God had no business creating the world. In other words, if God did not approve of, appreciate, and truly mean us to use our freedom, if he could have created by fiat, why didn't he just do it? A perfect world, just like that!

On the one hand, then, we have the tremendous conviction and feeling that God must know everything, must somehow or other foresee everything. And on the other hand we have the tremendous feeling that our freedom is real. The Scriptures provide exciting insights. Paul speaks about grace which is irrevocable; the call of God cannot be repented of (Rom. 11:29). On the other hand, he said if you do not repent you are going to perish (Rom. 2:4–5, 12, cf. Luke 13:3, 5)! Calvin taught predestination, and yet Brunner says that you do not find a single sermon

in which Calvin ever preached it. This is one of the real paradoxes
of life. Our problem is that we must somehow accept both foreknowledge and freedom.

I

Since a sovereign God of love must by his very nature create
responsibly, I believe that God knew and always has known
what he is doing and the end he is seeking. We must be more
sure of that as Christians than the Moslems, or the Marxists,
or anybody else. In this respect I am irretrievably a "supralap-
sarian" Calvinist. I believe without any question that all ultimate explanations and ultimate destinies must be referred to
God.

God has the sovereign initiative. From all eternity God knows
what he is doing. God then meant to create a general situation
where men must go their own way and must slowly find for
themselves that his way is best. In the fullness of time, when
all the preparation was done, he would come himself. That is,
God would come in his Son. He would enter history in the
fullness of his Spirit, in order to break down the separation,
in order to offer to freedom his love and our salvation.

God knew from all eternity that this was necessary. If he knew
from all eternity that it was necessary, he knew that the time
would have to come when in some individual, in his Son, there
would be a breakthrough of the understanding of his universal
love that had to be accepted in the freedom and faithfulness
of his fellowship. He also knew that there would be only a few
who would understand this reality, and they only distortedly
and partially. Far less would even those who did understand
accept this reality in the depths of their feelings.

People by their very nature are loyal to their own small ingroup because it makes them feel that they "belong." What
could be more difficult, then, than to identify oneself with
God's total purpose for all men? God knew from all eternity
that the Christ would not be received with understanding and
in the full meaning of his life. Nevertheless, God knew that
eventually the time would come when within the little living

ingroup of disciples someone would say, "No, we have to break down these barriers between us and others." Truth buried in sorrow will triumph tomorrow!

God did not come in Christ for the Jews alone. He came for the Gentiles. He came for all men. When this conviction came to Paul as it had come to Peter, he knew that he was completely within the sovereign initiative. Therefore James could say, in effect, "I know that God from all eternity has sanctioned what we are doing. What we are doing here is God's desire and not only our own will."

II

That is one side of the question of foreknowledge and freedom. Now what about the other side? A Christian must also believe that each person is responsibly free. God surely is not responsible for our sins. God surely is not responsible directly for our mistakes. If God is not responsible for our sins, for our mistakes, then certainly we have to accept the fact that there is such a thing as freedom, and that our freedom is real.

Now we are back on the other side again. Neither is our love and obedience simply God living in us. God may be more the subject of our lives than we are in one sense. But even though I believe that the relationship between God and man is that of co-subjects, so that the more God enters our life the more we become ourselves, I also believe that this does not happen until we understand and accept the will of God. When we are outside that will, we are, as Brunner said, unfree in one sense; we are free not to accept the will of God. Therefore our freedom is real too. We are real and free, our lives matter, and our freedom is significant. Paul's free acceptance of the gospel was important to human history.

I believe that God will never win, nor want to win, a victory that ever violates human freedom. I do not believe that God ever drags anybody into his kingdom. I do not believe that anyone is ever going to be saved by the devil's chasing him into heaven with a burning pitchfork. The most that fear can do is to frustrate man, and drive him to want to seek something that is more and other than himself. Romans 2 tells that it is only love that leads to repentance. Behold the severity and the goodness of God. It is the goodness of God that leads to repentance. Nevertheless severity is there in order to drive us to a choice, to make us willing to make a choice.

God respects, uses, yes, covets our freedom. Shall we say, then, that God calls the many, that God calls all? He would not be sovereign love if he did not call all. But only those are chosen who will understand and accept his will. God chooses the accepters. The invitation could not come apart from God, nor the will and the power to accept unless God had created us and made us for himself. Nonetheless there is in every human being the power to say no to God, to be free from God. The most amazing thing in the world is that we are free from God.

We may think of God as like a wise mother who puts lots of delicious cookies in a cookie jar, then leaves the kitchen, thus creating a moral situation for the child. God is not like a mother who stands over the child and says, "I dare you to take a cookie!" Nor is God like a mother who says, "I have counted every cookie; you can't get away with a thing." But if God just generously produces these moral situations, whereby he deliberately does not directly observe us all the time in order to create the indirect situation where in our ignorance we think we can ultimately "get away with things," then we are morally free.

The Christian must then put these two assertions together in faith; God works in terms of prevenient grace; and God works in terms of creative responsibility. Thus ultimately all things are to be referred to God.

III

On the other hand, all that happens proximately demands our choices. We cannot ultimately thwart God's will, but neither will God's will ever be done until we make it our own. God can know and control all that happens. He knows all that happens because when it happens it is there. But God does not know the undetermined future because the undetermined future is

not. It is "irreal." It is not real. It could have been but it never
became. God does not know mechanically as though he were
an astronomer predicting an eclipse. God does not know in the
sense that everything that is happening was meant to have
happened, as though God had produced a movie that he could
just roll out in human history that was already made. Rather,
God knows the future creatively. God knows the future as *you*
make the decisions and he knows what to do with all the decisions, because he is ultimately in control. In this cybernetic
relationship, this flexible feedback relationship, our freedom is
real but God's freedom is even more real.

God has the resources, God has the love, God has the possibility to have you in the hollow of his hand. You can trust God,
trust the sovereign initiative of God, the ultimate predestination of God. *But that predestination will never through all
eternity violate the responsibility and the freedom of man.*
From all eternity God has called you. Yes, you, each individual.
God has called you from all eternity to be a member of his
own life. God has called you to a fulfillment that is impossible
for any one of us to imagine. It is up to each one of us to be
continually accepting and entering into this relationship.

Human history stands on the verge of a new era. The only
way history can now move is in the direction of a qualitative
difference in terms of which we have a new genesis, a Christo-
genesis, a fulfillment as universal men and women able to face
the problems of the new age with power. We cannot face them
if we go on in our old nature. We must be reconstituted, we
must be reoriented, we must be remotivated. God has called
us from all eternity today to become new men and women by
a power and a grace which we cannot now imagine, because
it will make a qualitative difference in our lives. We will become not only the harbingers, not only the proclaimers, but
actually the reconstituters, the bringers of his new age.

God knew from all eternity what he was doing in the Council
of Jerusalem. God has known from all eternity what he is doing
in calling you to a new life, in calling you to a new hope, in
calling you to a new fulfillment. May you enter into it. Those
are indeed chosen who accept the sovereign will of God.

21.

Christian Hope

Hope does not disappoint us, because God's love has been poured into our hearts through the Holy Spirit which has been given to us. Romans 5:5.

OF ALL THE MAJOR religions, only the Christian faith gives full substance to hope. None of the pagan philosophies or non-Christian religions offers the kind of hope that the Christian faith gives. Certainly there is hope in other religions. But the Christian hope is unique with respect to the fulfillment of hope.

Several years ago I had an interesting talk with Rudolf Bultmann, one of Europe's great theologians. I wanted to make sure that my interpretation of his theology was correct, so I confronted him boldly and precisely on various issues. One question was that of life eternal or life after death. I knew that Dr. Bultmann refused to accept this as an aspect of his faith. I kept urging him, "Is it not possible for us, at least in a classical Christian sense, to accept life after death in some genuine way as part and parcel of the Christian faith?"

He puffed harder and harder on his pipe. Friends had told me that I had better not try his patience too much or he would show me the door, and that the pipe was a warning signal. But I persisted, "Dr. Bultmann, don't you really think that—putting aside your understanding of science, the modern mood, existentialism and all the rest—eternal life really is part of the

Christian faith?" He said, "No." Then he added, "But of course you can always hope. A person can hope anything."

I pondered this for a long time afterward. I take hope more seriously than my friend Rudolf Bultmann does. I do not believe that you have a right to hope *anything*. Hope is an important word. When Paul says that he lives in hope of the resurrection from the dead (Phil. 3:11), he is not talking lightly. He risked his life, he risked all that he was doing on the hope of the resurrection from the dead. Paul wrote that experience —suffering, endurance, character—brings hope and hope "maketh not ashamed," "does not disappoint us" (Rom. 5:3–5, KJV, RSV). An earned hope was far from being just something that everybody could have because he has the right to hope anything.

I

Hope is the expectant edge of faith. Hope makes faith concrete. Hope gives faith specific content. For example, I have *faith* that my wife loves me when I go away. But I *hope* she will write a letter. That is something concrete. Or a girl might say, "I trust Tommy, but I hope he will propose tonight." Thus, I have faith in God, but I hope that somehow we can have world peace. That is something concrete, something specific. Faith is a general attitude of trust and acceptance, but hope is something specific. As Milton says in *Paradise Lost*, "Hope never comes/That comes to all." * He does not mean that we cannot all have some great hope. But he means that hope always comes in a specific way to specific people. It comes concretely, it comes to you in a particular setting.

Hope is never mere wishing. When Bultmann says, "Of course you can hope that there is life after death because you can hope for anything," he is really taking lightly the word "hope." Hope comes out of experience. Hope is never mere wishing; experience alone works hope. It is based upon the character of the person, or the nature of the situation. But hope always comes in a tangible, concrete, personalized fashion. Neither is hope

* Book I, line 65.

merely having or seeing. The Bible rightly tells us that seen hope is no hope. Visible hope is no hope at all. Hope is thus the unpredictable, the free, the unprovable. Hope is the expectant edge of faith in which we must live if we are going to live fully.

But hope must always be warranted. Mere wishful thinking is not hope. Hope that is warranted, based upon experience, "does not disappoint us." We have faith in God, we have faith in his promises, but we never know how that promise is going to become true. Our answer to prayer comes in a concrete form whenever it comes.

To be hopeless is a terrible thing. It is true that the reason most people do so little is that they have so little hope; they think so little can be done. To be hopeless is to be cowed, sterile, self-defeated. In order to hope we have to expect. Francis Bacon said that hope is a good breakfast but a poor supper.

Hope is the expectant edge of faith. Furthermore, the ground of hope is God. "Hope in God," says the forty-second Psalm, "for I shall again praise him, my help and my God." Or in the first chapter of 1 Peter we read that our hope may be in God, because God can be trusted unconditionally—or all-conditionally. Hope is justified in general, but never in the specific. God will answer in his way. Therefore, you hope for specific things and God may show you that you may get something else which is quite different. It may take you some time to understand that what you hoped for was really answered. God will fill all your needs and give you all joy and peace in believing as you *abound in hope* in the power of the Holy Spirit.

When God is the ground of hope, we are on solid ground. Therefore we can "hope against hope" and know that hope does not disappoint us. Our particular hope may disappoint us —and how often we have been disappointed. To some, life is one disappointment after another. Many promises which seem near to fulfillment are suddenly snatched away. We begin to feel that before any good thing comes true it will be snatched away. But God always puts something else in its place, if we learn to understand his will. Hopes can disappoint us, but not hope in the final sense, only hope in the specific sense.

"You meant evil," said Joseph, "but God meant it for good" (Gen. 50:20). The worst thing that could happen to him turned out to be the best thing that could happen. God even becomes our hope as the ground of our being. "Christ in you the hope of glory." No hope is so true as when Christ becomes the center of our lives. What we really expect of life, and hope of life, is Christ's will in us. Therefore we can rejoice in hope already.

The poet Pope says that hope springs eternal in the human breast.* "All My Hope on God Is Founded" is one of the great hymns of the Christian church. The end of hope is either to be disappointed and disillusioned and to end in bitterness of spirit, or to find that open-ended hope, trusting God, which never disappoints. Experience works hope and hope does not disappoint us.

I like cynical people because cynical people are people who care. They have something in their hearts which is eating away. They would like things to be different and therefore at least they care. In this respect they are better than the superficial, indifferent people who do not care. I can get next to people if they are cynical, if they are bitter, if they are disappointed, because I know that they have had high hopes and they have been disillusioned. The fuller and better thing is to learn to find a hope that does not disappoint because it is not the prediction of our own will or our own prevision or our own understanding, but it is rather the acceptance of the kind of hope where everything that God gives works out for good to those who love him.

II

The main Christian hope is the hope in life eternal. We must trust God. It is more important to know in whom we believe than to know in what we believe. One of my dear friends used to come to me with all kinds of theological questions. Finally she began to ask me about life after death. I said, "To

---

* "Essay on Man," Epistle I, line 95.

be honest with you, I can't settle all those questions." She said,
"I want to *know*." I said, "I trust God, but I cannot spell out
all these things." Even though she was an educated person she
eventually joined a sect that claimed to be able to give all the
answers. She said, "I have to know exactly what happened on
the other side."

Well, I do not. I am not going to be disappointed, because
when I get on the other side, I am going to enter into my
Father's presence and my Father's promises. I am going to know
that what he gives is better than anything I could have pre-
dicted, imagined, or understood. His ways are bound to be reliable and to be good. Therefore I trust God for life after
death.

Another friend says that all the planets that God made are
out in space in order that when we get through life on this
planet we can go to another one for more education. It is going to be a wonderful thing going from one to the other for
more entering into the promises of God. That is a wonderful
hope to have. It is a beautiful hope my friend has, but I am
not at all positive about it. We may find out that what God
has for us is something else that is even better. The fundamental thing in Christian hope is *the expectant edge*. You must
have concrete hopes and live in them, nourish them, thank God
for them. But do not put your heart and mind on a specific
hope; put your heart and mind and trust in God. Then let
the hope be realized as it may be, and you will not be disappointed in the reality of God.

III

Let us not trim down the Bible's promises. In the Revised
Standard Version, for instance, there are several changes I do
not like. I suffer over some of the retranslations because they
trim down the theological promises and the relevance of the incarnation. Every translation naturally has within it its human
background and its human elements. The King James Version
translates 1 Corinthians 15:19 as "If in this life only we have
hope in Christ, we are of all men most miserable." We have

hope beyond this life. The context is completely obvious and evident. Hope is not limited to this life. We have endured all things, but our hope is going to be realized in God's way. The RSV reads, "If in this life we . . . have only hope." Apparently the translators do not want to connect hope with the next life. The old version says something far greater: If in this life only we have hope, then of all men we are most miserable.

I believe more and more that either we have to let our faith grow and grow in ever richer and deeper dimensions and in a fuller understanding of God—so that all our learning, all our discovery, becomes synthesized in a new and greater union and a fuller, truer religion in line with that universal will of God— or else we are going to lose the cutting edge, the expectant edge of faith. Therefore it will not do to try to trim down the faith in the interest of integrity. That kind of integrity is not the integrity of truth, though it is meant to be. It is, rather, the integrity of a loss of nerve for faith. We must let our faith and knowledge grow more and more into a vaster understanding of God. With Hosea we can call hope "a door" (Hos. 2:15). What a wonderful expression! Let us use the door! Let us pass through it to the fulfillment of the "lively hope" expressed in 1 Peter 1:3 (KJV), "a lively hope by the resurrection of Jesus Christ from the dead."

Zechariah uses the expression, "ye prisoners of hope" (Zech. 9:12, KJV). I want to live my life as God's prisoner of hope, in the sense that the more I experience and the more validly and adequately I interpret my experience, the more honest I am, the more I enter into life, the more I find that I have reached a freedom, a fullness in which I am a prisoner of hope. I cannot get away from it. I cannot get outside of hope. No matter how I try to get away from hope, it surrounds me; no matter what paths I pursue, hope is there.

I pray that you all find the great freedom that is a warranted hope, a hope that does not disappoint us, a hope that is a true hope. "Hope in God, for we shall again praise him, our help and our God." God bless you to enter this day into the fuller and truer hope.